THE PRICE GUIDE TO GOOD WINE

W9-BTH-979

Addison-Wesley Publishing Company
Reading, Massachusetts • Menlo Park, California
London • Amsterdam • Don Mills, Ontario • Sydney

Designed by K. C. Witherell
Set in 9 point Bodoni

Produced by Smallwood & Stewart, 156 Fifth Avenue,
New York 10010
ISBN 0-201-11381-3
ABCDEFGHIJ-IA-86543

CONTENTS

1
INTRODUCTION

If the message of this book can be summed up, it is that good wine is not necessarily expensive, nor are all cheap wines poor.

The wine buyer in America today has a choice of wines that is unmatched almost anywhere in the world. Visit an established Bordeaux wine merchant and you may find an extensive cellar and many rare vintages, but there will be few wines from Burgundy, Alsace, or the Loire on his shelves; fewer still from Germany or Italy; and very likely, none at all from the United States. Yet even a neighborhood liquor store will carry a range of these wines. In recent years, this has become a wealth of choice which the strength of the dollar has brought within reach of any wine buyer.

Most local liquor stores carry about twenty or so different white wines, varying in style from a sweet French Sauternes to a light California Chablis to a robust Rioja *reserva*, and ranging in price from about $3 to $20 or $30 a bottle. This profusion of labels can be both a delight and a source of confusion.

The Price Guide to Good Wine aims to take some of the mystery and a lot of the chance out of choosing between these and other wines. Country-by-country, six noted wine authorities have contributed their expert advice on buying wine. They have selected and recommended nearly 300 wines as good value-for-money under these price categories: Under $5; $5–$10; $10–$15; Over $15.

A book such as this cannot be comprehensive, but it does cover the most important wine-producing countries and most of the major styles of wine sold in the United States. A certain amount of snobbery, combined with effective marketing, has meant that some good wines fetch high prices while others, though just as good, sell for only a fraction of the cost. Many of these 'undiscovered' bargains are listed here, together with advice on buying to help you distinguish between wines that really are good value and those that are not.

HOW TO USE THIS BOOK

To make this guide as practical as possible it has been organized around the information you are presented with on the label. Each wine-producing country is described separately with a glossary of its common wine terms, and the alphabetical listing of selected wines that follows has been arranged so that a wine entry can be found easily in a crowded liquor store.

Except where indicated, these wines are widely available. Because of regional variations in distribution and marketing, it may be that a wine listed in the Under $5 category, for example, is priced at a dollar or two more. In this case (unless it is marked as a best buy) you should probably pass it over.

1. Wine headings
Wines appear under the name that is most prominent on the label. Where relevant, recommended producers or shippers are listed at the end of the entry.

2. Regions
Where of particular relevance, region of origin is given.

3. Vintages
Not all wines are vintaged. Recommended vintages are given for those that are; years suitable for drinking now are underlined thus: 80

4. Best Buys
All the wines included in this book are recommended. Some offer exceptional value and these "best buys" are indicated by a ★.

THE WINES OF *France*

The wines of France have enjoyed the greatest reputation and offer the greatest variety of styles of any wines in the world. Commercially known for hundreds of years, French wines have been categorized, analyzed, memorized, and lionized.

While not every wine producer in the world might agree that French wines have set the standards by which all other wines are judged, it certainly must be acknowledged that French wine types have become a kind of "shorthand" to describe a wine's style. The names *Burgundy, Bordeaux,* and *Rhône,* for example, are used on wine labels all over the world because they conjure up specific taste memories.

This great variety may account for the fact that over 60 percent of French wines in the United States are from specific wine regions. Foreign imports from other countries normally show a majority of lower level wines without regional designations.

READING THE LABEL

The *Appellation d'Origine Contrôlée* (AC) regulations are the basis of the French wine laws. The best French wines and most of the bottles exported meet AC requirements, and on any label they are the first words to look for. Principally, these regulations guarantee the origin of the wine— an AC region anywhere in size from a few acres to an area as large as Bordeaux— and this is usually bracketed on the label by the words "Appellation" and "Contrôlée." In addition, AC controls the grape varieties, the location of vineyards and types of soil, the minimum alcohol that a wine must have, the maximum amount that can be produced, and other viticultural and vinicultural practices. But while AC guarantees the authenticity of the contents of the bottle, it does not necessarily guarantee quality.

As the regions get smaller, the regulations get stricter, and the wines are of a higher quality. Thus a wine carrying the appellation Médoc, or better still a township in the Médoc, almost certainly will be superior to one carrying the general Bordeaux appellation. The largest AC region can produce wine from several grape varieties, with a moderate amount of alcohol. In the next smaller area the allowable grape varieties are reduced, and the minimum alcohol is increased; production is also decreased, in order to maintain quality. Finally, the very

smallest areas have to meet the highest standards. In Bordeaux, this highest level of AC is the township; in Burgundy, it is a *Grand Cru* vineyard.

VDQS (*Vins Délimités de Qualité Supérieure*) is used for quality wines produced in accordance with government regulations that are not entitled to AC labelling.

The second piece of information to look for is the name of the producer or shipper. The wine may have a single producer who grows the grapes and vinifies and bottles the wine. Such a wine is "estate bottled" and includes the producer's name on the label. Often a wine is the product of many vineyards, and it is the *négociant*, or shipper, who buys different lots of wine to make up a blend. In this case, the shipper's name would appear on the label. Wines sold in the United States must have the name of the importer as well.

In addition, a wine label may have the name of a château or vineyard. One French law states that anything that appears on a label must be 100 percent. Thus, if a grape variety is mentioned, there will be 100 percent of that grape used. The same holds for a vintage year.

While the contents of the bottle must be listed, the percent of alcohol does not, since United States laws recognize the AC laws regarding minimum alcohol content.

There are a great number of French wines that travel under a brand name, and are simply labelled "Product of France." This category is known as *vin de table*. They generally do not have vintage dates, and the regions that the grapes come from are not revealed. The négociant must list his address with a code number, so that the consumer will not be misled into thinking that the négociant's address is the same as the origin of the wine. Thus, this large category of wines is unofficially known as "zip code wines."

The wine-growing regions of France are the most diverse of any country. Some familiarity with the general characteristics of their individual wines and a little knowledge of the geography of the regions are essential to learning about French wine.

Two regions are most famous for still wines: Bordeaux and Burgundy. Most of the world-renowned white and red French wines that command top prices are produced in these two areas, together with a great deal of good reds and whites and everyday table wines. Beaujolais, Rhône, Provence, the Loire Valley, and Alsace are also wine-producing regions of importance with distinctive wines.

About a quarter of French imports are from the Bordeaux region in southwestern France, equally divided between red and white. Geographically, the Gironde River and its tributaries, the Garonne and Dordogne, help to separate the wine regions or *communes* of Bordeaux. Within the limits

of the Bordeaux appellation there are about 20 major communes. A producer of AC wines within any of these regions will use the more precise appellation rather than the general Bordeaux label, which is normally reserved for blends. A further refinement is the 300 or so major châteaux within these regions that account for the very finest wines from Bordeaux. They are sold under the name of the château and are usually estate bottled. Most of the châteaux are located in the main communes of Médoc, Graves, Sauternes, Pomerol, and St.-Emilion.

Bordeaux's famous wines are mainly reds, which are made from cabernet sauvignon, merlot, petit verdot, and some malbec grapes. Red Bordeaux wines traditionally have a lot of tannin which helps them last a long time; many reach their best after several years aging.

The important white grapes of Bordeaux are the sauvignon blanc and the sémillon. Sauvignon blanc produces rich, dry wines. Under proper conditions, the sémillon grape is infected with *pourriture noble* (noble mold) which gives the wine a special sweetness and concentration. These golden wines, known as Sauternes, are the most famous whites from Bordeaux.

Burgundy accounts for 15 percent of the French wines in the United States, with whites leading reds by two to one. The important white grape of Burgundy is the

chardonnay, which is particularly successful in chalky soil. Red Burgundies are produced from the pinot noir grape. Burgundies
have a reputation for being rich, full-bodied
wines, but in fact they are generally much
more delicate than most people realize, and
less long-lived than Bordeaux reds because
they have less tannin.

Beaujolais and the Rhône, to the south
of Burgundy, are the next most significant
areas. The wines of Beaujolais, made from
the gamay grape, are fruity and light. Rhône
wines, farther south, are mainly from the
grenache and syrah grapes. These reds tend
to be full-bodied and achieve high alcohol.
The Rhône is also the home of a notable
rosé, Tavel.

Provence, also in the south, produces
dry, spicy wines, especially the rosés.

The Loire region, along the six hundred
mile Loire River, produces a variety of
wines; white Muscadet in the west, Pouilly-
Fumé and Sancerre in the east, and rosés
from Anjou, as well as reds and whites in
the center of the region.

Alsace, in northeastern France, is separated from Germany by the Rhine River.
Its wines are often coupled with those from
Germany, and while there are some similarities—the same grapes are used, for
example—the style is much drier and the
French wines are often aged in wood.

GLOSSARY OF TERMS

appellation d'origine contrôlée (AC)–term on French wine labels that guarantees origin.

blanc–white.

blanc de blancs–wine made from the juice of white grapes only.

château bottled–wine bottled at the château where grapes from which it was made were grown, usually Bordeaux.

commune–a subdivision of a district, sometimes known as a parish.

cru–a vineyard or growth.

cru classé–a classified growth, such as the 1855 of Bordeaux. The number of the growth—first, second, and so on—is no certain guide to quality.

cuvée–a blend of wines.

estate bottled–wine produced and bottled by the vineyard owner-producer.

goût de terroir–taste imparted by the soil.

growth– see *cru* and *cru classé*.

mise au domaine–phrase on labels designating estate bottling, usually in Burgundy.

mise en bouteille au château–same as above, usually in Bordeaux.

négociant–merchant who buys wine from a grower; blends, bottles, and markets it.

rouge–red.

vin de table–French table wine.

vins délimités de qualité supérieure(VDQS)– category of French wines that do not quite merit AC, but still conform to government regulations.

Albert Lucas
Vin de Table

This set of three nonappellation wines is medium-bodied and dry. The red is like a Beaujolais, and the white has some Chardonnay with a touch of wood. The rosé is also quite dry.

B&G Light
Vin de Table

This blanc de blancs white wine is both low alcohol and low calorie (about one third less than most dry white wines). It is crisp and fruity with hints of apples and citrus.

★ **Barsac**
Bordeaux
78

This wine is named for one of the five communes of the Sauternes district, where the famous sweet wines of France are produced. The regional wine is one of the most reasonably priced from any shipper.
Shipper: Alfred Schyler Fils & Co.

Beaujolais
Burgundy
82, 81

The Beaujolais district is south of the Côte d'Or, planted with the gamay grape. The red wines are light and fruity and drinkable with no further aging.
Shippers: B&G St. Louis, Sichel Reserve de l'Abbé

Beaujolais-Villages
Burgundy
82, 81

Fruity red wine that may come from any of 39 villages that are the best of northern Beaujolais. The standards are higher than those for Beaujolais.
See Wines $5–10.
Shippers: Château de Lacarelle, Chanson St. Vincent, Mommessin La Belle Côte

Boucheron
Vin de Table
These dry, nonappellation wines are available in blanc de blancs and cuvée rouge. They are medium-bodied and consistent.

Champmorond
Vin de Table
Another of France's table wines whose blend is the producer's choice. The white is very light and dry; the red is slightly fuller in body.

Chanson Select
Vin de Table
These dry yet fruity table wines have some character, even without a specific appellation on the label. Both white and red are good wines.

Château Lauretan
Bordeaux Supérieur
<u>79</u> (red); <u>81</u> (white)
This is a good petit château that produces both red and white wines. Supérieur means that the standards are slightly higher than other Bordeaux.

★ **Chevalier de Vedrines**
Bordeaux
<u>79</u> (red);
<u>82</u>, <u>81</u>, <u>80</u> (white)
Exceptional dry wines from Bordeaux. The white is produced from sauvignon blanc grapes only, without any of the usual mix of sémillon.

Claude Mercier
Vin de Table
A dry, crisp white blanc de blancs and a dry, balanced red comprise these nonappellation table wines.

Côtes-du-Rhône
Rhône
<u>81</u>, <u>80</u>, <u>79</u>
Red wines from designated areas of the Rhône Valley, these are often in a fruity Beaujolais style but sometimes very spicy with a lot of Rhône character.
Producers: B&G, Bouchard Père, Chanson, Delas (St. Esprit), Dom. de Renjardière, Ponnelle

Côtes-du-Rhône Blanc
Rhône
82, 81

A very small amount of white wine is produced in the Côtes-du-Rhône region, helping to fill the demand for dry, inexpensive French wines.
Producers: David & Foillard, Marquis de Simiane, Delas (St. Esprit)

Crozes-Hermitage Blanc
Rhône
80

Crozes-Hermitage surrounds the famous Hermitage hillside in the northern Rhône. Even though lower priced than Hermitage, Crozes-Hermitages are no longer as inexpensive as they used to be. This is a good find. See Wines $5–10.
Shipper: Bouchard Père

Crustaces Alsace
Alsace

Alsace vinifies its wines in a drier style than the nearby wines of Germany. This proprietary wine is blended to accompany seafood.
Producer: Dopff & Irion

Cuvée Lupe-Cholet
Vin de Table

This fine old Burgundy firm has produced a good pair of blanc and rouge nonappellation dry table wines.

Cuvée Vercherre
Vin de Table

These dry table wines are from a producer based in the Rhône. The white has surprisingly full flavor not hinted at by its very light color.

Eclat
Vin de Table

Eclat's proprietary labeling allows the blanc de blancs to come from Entre-Deux-Mers in Bordeaux, and the rouge to come from the Gigondas area in the Rhône. Both are fruity and dry.

Grande Marque
Bordeaux
79, 78 (red);
80, 79 (white)

Blended from less expensive regions of Bordeaux, the white is flowery and off-dry, and the red is soft and drinkable. **Shipper: Dourthe Frères**

Jaboulet Rouge Le Table du Roy
Vin de Table

Jaboulet Aîné is an old firm from the Rhône, producing rich, flavorful red wines. This non-appellation wine is a well-priced example.

La Cour Pavillon
Bordeaux
78, 76 (red);
80, 79 (white)

Proprietary wine from LaCour in Bordeaux, the wines are blended to be very drinkable. The red can take some age.

La Forêt
Burgundy
82, 81

A deservedly popular proprietary white wine from Drouhin in Burgundy that is crisp and dry, with good acidity.

Le Jardinet
Vin de Table

One of the best values in white table wines, this blanc de blancs is fruity and nicely-balanced.

★ **Maître d'Estournel**
Bordeaux
79 (red);
82, 81 (white)

A fresh, fruity white wine blended from sauvignon blanc and sémillon grapes by Prats Frères, proprietors in Bordeaux.

Meribeau
Vin de Table

This blanc de blancs is a non-appellation table wine, but the rouge is a VDQS wine from the Côteaux de Languedoc. Its price and drinkability, though, place it nicely in the table wine category.

Moreau Blanc
Vin de Table

J. Moreau is a producer from Chablis, and this table wine is in his very dry, crisp style. A red is also available.

Muscadet
Loire
<u>82</u>, <u>81</u>, <u>79</u>

Muscadet is a charming, dry white wine from the western end of the Loire. The best are not too acidic. See Wines $5–10. **Producers: Barré Frères, Remy-Pannier, Martin Frères**

Oliver de France
Bordeaux
<u>79</u> (red); <u>82</u>, <u>81</u> (white)

Eschenauer is still another Bordeaux proprietor who has created some fine blends. The white is fragrant, medium-dry with good, balancing acidity. The red is soft and drinkable.

Papillon de La Reine
Vin de Table

These blanc de blancs, rosé, and red wines from Dennis & Huppert are clean, fresh, and well-made.

Partarger
Vin de Table

B&G's appealing table wines are varied: the blanc is light, clean, and fresh, the vin rouge is medium-bodied and can be chilled, and the rosé is medium dry and delicate.

Remy-Pannier
Vin de Table

This producer has created inexpensive quaffing wines: Rouge de France, Blanc de France, and Rosé de France. They are quite drinkable.

Roland Thevenin
Vin de Table

Roland Thevenin has been dubbed the "Poet Laureate of Burgundy." He loyally uses grapes that grow in Burgundy for his nonappellation red and white. Both are fruity and dry.

Rosé d'Anjou
Loire
<u>82</u>, <u>81</u>, <u>80</u>, <u>79</u>

Among the most popular wines of France are the semidry rosés from Anjou, in the center of the Loire Valley. They are very

brilliant with a light pink color.
Producers: Duplessis-Mornay,
Lichine, Moc Baril, Remy-
Pannier, Tytel

Sichel Cuvée Special
Vin de Table

Cuvée Special Blanc blends
fruity wines from Bordeaux and
the Loire to create a light,
medium-dry white wine. The
Cuvée Special Rouge is a fruity
wine from southern Rhône. It
can be chilled.

Tavel Rosé
Rhône Valley
79, 78

One of France's driest rosés
comes from Tavel, in the southern Rhône. This one, from
Bellicard d'Avignon, is a best
buy. See Wines $5–10.

★ Valbon
Vin de Table

Bouchard Père, a producer of
both Burgundy and Rhône
wines, has made a Valbon white
wine which is quite dry, with
good fruit. Valbon red is an
exceptional vin de table with
the rich flavors of the Rhône,
softened by the gamay grape of
Beaujolais. The rosé is dry.

Vouvray
Loire
82, 81

Vouvray, in the center of the
long Loire Valley, is known
for fragrant, medium-dry wines
made from the chenin blanc
grape. This one, from Remy-
Pannier, is a good example at
this price. See Wines $5–10.

Wan Fu
Vin de Table

Wan Fu was created by shipper Sichel to accompany aromatic foods. It is a semidry
white wine, which goes well
with Indian and Chinese food.

Bandol Rosé
Provence
<u>81</u>, <u>80</u>
Here is a dry, spicy rosé from the southern, sunny region of Provence. This cuvée marine from Domaine Ott is especially good with fish stews.

Beaujolais Blanc
Burgundy
<u>82</u>
A small percentage of wine from Beaujolais is white, and it is similar to Pouilly-Fuissé and Mâcon Blanc. Dry and crisp.
Producers: Beaudet, Jadot, Maufoux

Beaujolais-Villages
Burgundy
<u>82</u>, <u>81</u>, <u>80</u>
The popular, fruity red wine may come from the 39 best villages of Beaujolais, and may be aged a little, if desired.
See Wines Under $5.
Producers: Beaudet, Bouchard, Drouhin, Duboeuf, Jadot, Latour, Maufoux, Marquisat, Ponnelle

Bourgogne Rouge
Burgundy
<u>79</u>, <u>78</u>
A regional red wine from Burgundy, whose producers are established firms in the area. Try Faively's Chevaliers du Tastevin and Latour's Cuvée Latour

★ **Chablis**
Burgundy
<u>82</u>, <u>81</u>
Popular wine from the region between northern Burgundy and Paris, famous for very crisp, dry white wines.
Producers: B&G, Chanson St. Vincent, Maufoux, Moreau, Pic

Chablis Premier Cru
Burgundy
<u>82</u>, <u>81</u>
Chablis from selected vineyards, which may or may not be mentioned on the label, are known as Premier Cru. Only the Grand Cru vineyards are rated higher. Famous Premier Cru vineyards are: Fourchaumes, Vaillons, and Montmains.
See Wines $10–15.

Producers: Bouchard, Regnard, Remy-Pannier, Vocoret

Chardonnay
Burgundy
82, 80, 78

The grape of white Burgundy, its name appears on the label only when the wine comes from the Mâcon district, and only Chardonnay grapes are used. **Producers:** B&G St. Louis, Moreau, Sichel Reserve de l'Abbé

Château Coufran
Haut-Médoc,
Bordeaux
79, 78

A Cru Grand Bourgeois château that has a reputation for value and consistency. The wines are drinkable early.

Château de la Chaize
Burgundy
82

One of the largest and most impressive châteaux in Brouilly, which is one of the best districts of Beaujolais. The wines are quite fruity, and can age well. Also try the Brouilly from Domaine Geoffray.

Château Greysac
Médoc,
Bordeaux
80, 79

Another Cru Grand Bourgeois château that is widely known, with flavorful wines. This one is from northern Médoc.

Château La Garde
Graves,
Bordeaux
80, 79

A château in the Graves district, in the south of Bordeaux. The red is very fruity, with some berry characteristics.

★**Château Larose-Trintaudon**
Haut-Médoc,
Bordeaux
79, 78

This Cru Grand Bourgeois provides excellent value, coupling fine wines with good supply. These reds are dry and rich.

Château Ste. Roseline
Provence
79, 78

A Provençal château, famous for its rosé wines. They are dry and spicy, with some length.

★ Châteauneuf-
du-Pape
Rhône
81, 80, 79

Site of the summer palace of the pope at Avignon, where very rich, high-alcohol, tannic red wines are produced.
Shippers: B&G, Bouchard

Côte-Rôtie
Rhône
75, 74

One of the best regions of northern Rhône, with very steep vineyards. The wines are rich and slightly peppery.
Producers: Delas Frères, Domaine Gerin, Jaboulet-Vercherre

Crozes-
Hermitage
Blanc
Rhône
80, 79, 78

A small percentage of Crozes-Hermitage wines are white, and they are very dry and flavorful.
Producers: Chapoutier Les Meysonniers, Jaboulet Mule Blanche, Tain L'Hermitage

Crozes-
Hermitage
Rouge
Rhône
80, 79, 78, 77, 76

Rhône wines from 11 districts around the Hermitage hillside are rich in fruit and alcohol and are less expensive than Hermitage. See Wines $10–15.
Producers: Chapoutier Les Meysonniers, Jaboulet Domaine de Thalabert, Larive

Fonset Lacour
Bordeaux
79 (red); 80 (white)

B&G has produced these good, drinkable Bordeaux blends. The blanc is crisp and dry, and the rouge is fruity and smooth.

★ Gewürz-
traminer
Alsace
81, 79

A perfumed white wine of Alsace, made from the grape of the same name. It is very dry, with the scent of lichees.
Producers: Dopff, Dopff & Irion, Hugel, Klug, Trimbach, Willm

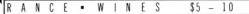

Gigondas
Rhône
_79_, _78_

Red wine from southern Rhône, with high alcohol but less tannin than the neighboring Châteauneuf-du-Pape.
Producers: Bellicard d'Avignon, Caves des Vignerons, Maufoux

Graves
Bordeaux
_81_, _80_, _79_, _78_

Regional white wine from a district in Bordeaux, with very fruity whites made from the sauvignon blanc and sémillon.
Producers: Sichel, Ginestet, Baron Philippe de Rothschild

Mâcon Blanc
Burgundy
_82_

The Mâconnais is the home of the famous Pouilly-Fuissé, whose production limitations cannot supply the demand. Nearby, Mâcon whites are good alternates.
Shippers: B&G, Bouchard, Jadot

Mâcon-Lugny
Les Charmes
Burgundy
_82_, _81_

Lugny is a district in Mâcon producing fine white wines from the chardonnay grape. One of the best vineyards is Les Charmes.

Mâcon-Villages
Burgundy
_82_, _81_, _80_

White wines from certain communes in Mâcon are entitled to the name Mâcon-Villages. They often are not more expensive than Mâcon Blanc.
Producers: Latour, Le Grand Chéneau, Marquisat, Maufoux

Margaux
Bordeaux
_81_

A regional red wine from one of the important communes of Haut-Médoc. This one from Alfred Schyler Fils is an exceptional value.

Médoc
Bordeaux
<u>81</u>, <u>79</u>, 78

Many important châteaux wines come from the Médoc, so a regional red wine blend from this area is always of interest.
Shippers: B&G, Baron Philippe de Rothschild, Borie Manoux, Prats, Schyler, Sichel

Mouton Cadet
Bordeaux
nonvintage (red);
<u>80</u> (white)

Famous for his own prestigious château, the Baron Philippe de Rothschild lends his name to these good regional blends. The blanc is fresh and clean. The rouge cuvée is fruity.

Muscadet
Loire
<u>82</u>, <u>81</u>, <u>79</u>

Muscadet is a fresh, reliable wine, which can easily serve as an all-purpose white. The wine is dry with depth and charm.
See Wines Under $5.
Producers: B&G, Marquis de Goulaine, Metaireau, Monmousseau

Pouilly-Fuissé
Burgundy
<u>82</u>

Limited supply and increased demand have caused prices of the dry, white Pouilly-Fuissé to skyrocket. However, Alexis Lichine and Lupe-Cholot have held the line. See Wines $10–15.

Pouilly-Fumé
Loire
<u>82</u>, <u>81</u>, <u>79</u>

At the eastern end of the Loire Valley, the two major wines are Pouilly-Fumé and Sancerre, both bone-dry white wines.
See Wines $10–15.
Producers: Bailly, Chatelain Domaine de Saint-Laurent, Duplessis-Mornay, Redde, Remy-Pannier

Riesling
Alsace
<u>82</u>, <u>81</u>, <u>80</u>, <u>79</u>

Riesling lends itself to more ways of vinification than almost any other grape. Often made

sweet, the Alsatian wine is bone dry.
Producers: Dopff, Dopff & Irion, Hugel, Klug, Trimbach

St.-Emilion
Bordeaux
<u>81</u>, <u>80</u>, <u>79</u>, <u>78</u>
The regional blends in this famous red wine district often come from 8 adjoining towns. The reds are soft and early maturing.
Shippers: B&G, Baron Philippe de Rothschild, Schyler, Sichel

Sancerre
Loire
<u>82</u>, <u>81</u>, <u>80</u>
The wines of Sancerre are especially distinctive, as winemakers coax a lot of varietal character out of the sauvignon blanc grape.
Shippers: Archambault, Remy-Pannier, Redde

Sauternes
Bordeaux
<u>78</u>, <u>76</u>
Sauternes is a great, sweet white wine-producing district. Regional blends offer good values as compared to the more famous châteaux.
Shippers: B&G, Baron Philippe de Rothschild, Borie Manoux, Ginestet, Prats

Tavel Rosé
Rhône
<u>82</u>, <u>81</u>, <u>80</u>, <u>79</u>
These bone-dry, coral-hued wines prove that not all rosés are sweet. See Wines Under $5.
Producers: Château d'Aqueria, B&G, and Delas Frères

Vouvray
Loire
<u>82</u>, <u>81</u>, <u>80</u>
The chenin blanc grape, when grown along the Loire River, sometimes gets a rich, honey-like perfume and taste.
Shippers: B&G, Château de Montfort, Duplessis-Mornay Cuvée Florent

★ **Beaune-Grèves**
Burgundy
79
Les Grèves is one of the leading red wine vineyards in Beaune. The wine is dry with the famous *goût de terroir* or "taste of the soil." This, from Domaine P. de Marcilly, is an excellent value.

Chablis Grand Cru
Burgundy
81, 80, 79
The best Chablis comes from only 7 vineyards in that region, which are always named on the label. Vineyards most frequently seen in the United States are Blanchots, Les Clos, Valmur, and Les Preuses. The wine is dry and rich. See Wines $5–10.
Producers: Forgeot, Pic, Vocoret

Chassagne-Montrachet
Burgundy
80
This commune in the Côte de Beaune is famous for its white wines, even though many good reds come from the area as well. The whites are 100 percent chardonnay grapes. Mommessin is one producer offering this wine at a good price.

Château Loudenne
Médoc, Bordeaux
78
This elegant, fruity red wine comes from a château right on the Gironde River. Smaller amounts of an excellent white wine are also made.

Château Olivier
Graves, Bordeaux
81
This château in the Graves region produces a white wine that is dry and distinctive. The sauvignon blanc grape is quite varietal in character here.

Château Petit Village
Pomerol, Bordeaux
80
In Pomerol, wines are measured against Château Petrus, which is deservedly expensive. This château offers an excellent value from this red wine region,

26

especially in the less famous years.

Château Prieuré-Lichine
Margaux, Bordeaux
<u>80</u>

This château in Margaux has been receiving most favorable reviews in the last decade for its full, round red wines.

Château Simard
St.-Emilion, Bordeaux
<u>76</u>, <u>75</u>

This is one of the moderate-sized châteaux of St.-Emilion, producing red wines that age nicely.

Châteauneuf-du-Pape
Rhône
<u>80</u>, 79, <u>78</u>

From the most important wine district in southern Rhône come reds which have high alcohol and tannin. They are worth laying away. See Wines $5–10.
Producers: Chapoutier La Bernardine, Delas (St. Esprit), Domaine de Mont Redon, Jaboulet (Les Cedres), Maufoux

Châteauneuf-du-Pape Blanc
Rhône
<u>81</u>, <u>80</u>

Many of the producers of red Châteauneuf - du - Pape (see above) also make a small amount of white. While not produced from the familiar chardonnay grapes of Burgundy to the north, these wines are dry and rich, many in a Burgundian style.

Côte de Beaune-Villages
Burgundy
<u>79</u>, <u>78</u>

Red wines with this appellation may come from 16 different villages, which may or may not be on the label. Usually more famous areas, such as Santenay, will be listed.
Producers: Chanson, Jadot, Latour

Côte-Rôtie
Rhône
80, 79, <u>78</u>, <u>77</u>, <u>76</u>

The syrah grape gives this red northern Rhône wine its full, spicy character. Prices vary with vintages. Try Chapoutier and Domaine Gerin.

Hermitage
Rhône
80, 79, <u>78</u>, <u>77</u>, <u>76</u>

South of Côte-Rôtie is the Hermitage hillside, which also has excellent red wines filled with flavor and potential (see Châteauneuf-du-Pape, above).
Producers: Chapoutier M. de la Sizeranne, Delas (St. Christophe), Jaboulet, Maufoux

Hermitage
Blanc
Rhône
<u>80</u>, <u>79</u>, 78

As with the less expensive Crozes-Hermitage and also with Châteauneuf-du-Pape, small amounts of lovely, dry, white wines are produced in these predominantly red wine areas. The producers are the same as those listed above under Hermitage.

Meursault
Burgundy
<u>80</u>, 79

This commune in the Côte de Beaune is known for dry white wines that are delicate and softened with oak. Although these wines have become expensive, Pierre Matrot offers good value.

Muscat
Beaumes de
Venise
Rhône <u>81</u>
(often nonvintage)

One of the most perfumed white wines, this closely resembles the grape from which it is produced. This muscat wine is sweet and rich.
Shippers: Jaboulet, Maufoux

Pouilly-
Fuissé
Burgundy
<u>82</u>, 81

Although fame has made Pouilly-Fuissé more expensive than its neighbors, there are a few that are worth the

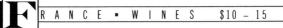
premium price.
Shippers: Chanson, Dom. Corsin, Jadot, Latour, Maufoux

Pouilly-Fumé The most important grape of
Château du the eastern end of the Loire
Nozet Valley is the sauvignon blanc.
Loire Ladoucette, the producer of this
82, 81 wine, has made a stylish example with the distinctive "grassy" varietal character of that grape.

WINES OVER $15

Château Cos This second growth château is
d'Estournel one of the best in St. Estèphe.
Haut-Médoc, It is known for its complex red
Bordeaux wines that take some time to
76 unfold. It is now owned by the Prats family.

Château From a third growth château
Giscours in Margaux, these red wines are
Haut-Médoc, a good lesson in the elegance
Bordeaux and perfume of the region at a
76 still affordable price.

Château Gruaud- Produced by one of the largest
Larose properties in St. Julien, this
Haut-Médoc, supple red wine is in reason-
Bordeaux ably good supply. It has been
79 classed a second growth, and is deservedly popular.

Château Haut- This highly praised château in
Bailly the Graves district produces red
Graves, wines of great balance. For a
Bordeaux time it was not so widely re-
79, 76 garded but today is sought after.

★ Château Suduiraut
Sauternes, Bordeaux
<u>79</u>

Sauternes, at their best, are honey-scented dessert wines, their ripeness enhanced by the pourriture noble. Château Suduiraut is a prime example of this style of wine.

Gevrey-Chambertin
Burgundy
<u>79</u>, <u>78</u>

Gevrey-Chambertin is a major commune in the Côte de Nuits known for its rich, earthy wines. Without a specific vineyard or producer, the quality of the wine depends on the shipper.
Shippers: B&G, Mommessin

Puligny-Montrachet
Burgundy
<u>81</u>, <u>80</u>, <u>79</u>

Many famous white wine vineyards come from this commune in the Côte de Beaune. Whether a single vineyard or regional wine, it is usually a very good example of what great white Burgundies should be.
Shippers: Chanson, Drouhin, Latour, Maufoux

Volnay Les Caillerets
Burgundy
<u>79</u>

Les Caillerets is one of the best and most famous red wine vineyards of Volnay, in the Côte de Beaune. It is a good example of Burgundian character, combining the best from the soil, pinot noir grapes, and aging in oak casks.
Shipper: Bouchard Père

THE
WINES
OF
ITALY

*A*s a producer of fine wines Italy is as yet largely undiscovered. Rather, it is best known for inexpensive everyday drinking wines—wines to quaff rather than to contemplate or take seriously.

Most Italian wines, of course, do fall in this category (as do most of the world's wines). But Italy produces much more than just plonk. Some of Italy's red wines, in particular, can stand alongside the best produced anywhere in the world. Given sufficient age, a Barbaresco, Chianti Classico riserva, or a Brunello di Montalcino, from a fine producer and vintage, can develop into a magnificent wine—noble in character with a depth and complexity of bouquet and flavor, excellent balance, and an intricate, lingering finish.

Italy's white wines do not reach the same heights; even the very best are no match for the finest whites from California or France. But Italy has made great strides in its white wines in the past few years, and we are now seeing many good Italian whites, some of which are very promising.

Whether through underestimation or neglect, Italy's better wines have generally commanded lower prices than their equivalents from France, and many bargains can be found.

It is difficult to make generalizations about Italian wines. Italian producers are more innovative than their French counterparts and are not hesitant to add new wines to their production or experiment with new styles; in this respect they are closer in spirit to American winemakers. For example, Valpolicella and the ubiquitous Soave, red and white wines respectively, are produced in both dry and sweet versions (and locally in a *spumante* too). Similarly, the barbera and grignolino grapes are used to produce not only reds but whites in some parts of Italy.

Some broad generalizations about Italian wine can be made. Comparatively, French wines tend to be firmer and leaner and California wines more alcoholic and fullbodied for equivalent types. Italy falls somewhere in between these two: combining the fruit and softness of the California style with the more moderate alcohol of the French.

In an attempt to impose some control over the quality of their wines, the Italian government introduced the DOC (*Denominazione di Origine Controllata*) system,

loosely modeled on the French *appellation
contrôlée* laws. Altogether over two hundred wines can be labelled DOC. But while
this reputedly guarantees that the wine you
are buying has been produced under controlled conditions, it is no certain guide to
quality. Many excellent wines, for one rea-
son or another, are sold only as *Vino da
Tavola*, a loose, all-embracing category
that includes a few of Italy's best and some
of her worst wines.

DOCG (*Denominazione di Origine Controllata e Garantita*) is a further refinement of the DOC system introduced in an
attempt to separate only the very best DOC
wines into a class of their own by even
closer restrictions. So far only four wines—
Barbaresco, Barolo, Brunello di Montalcino,
and Vino Nobile di Montepulciano—have
been granted this status.

In Italy, as in many other fine wine producing countries, you cannot judge a wine
by its region of origin or grape variety
alone; you must know something of the
producer and often the vintage as well.
Generally, the better and more expensive
the wine is, the more important this information is. Vintages vary enormously, and
producers perhaps even more so. For
example, while you can buy almost any
young Verdicchio or one of the several other
reliable everyday wines produced in Italy
and not go too far wrong, the same is definitely not so for a Brunello di Montalcino

or Barolo, where you must be much more selective to avoid disappointment.

READING THE LABEL

An Italian wine label may tell you a lot or a little about the wine in the bottle. The least it will say is the name of the wine, the name of the producer or bottler, where the wine was bottled, its category of regulation (*Vino da Tavola*, DOC, DOCG, etc.), and the quantity of wine in the bottle.

Italian wines are named in a few different ways: in the entries that follow, most are place names or grape names, or a combination of the two; occasionally they are proprietary or fantasy names.

GLOSSARY OF TERMS

abboccato–lightly sweet, somewhat less so than *amabile*.

alcool–alcohol.

amabile–semisweet.

bianco–white.

cannellino–sweet.

chiaretto–rosé.

classico–from the traditional part of the production zone, often, but not necessarily, the best.

consorzio–voluntary growers association formed to protect and promote the reputation of their wine; not an indication of quality, although their standards are frequently higher than DOC.

Denominazione di Origine Controllata(DOC)–
controlled denomination of origin. The set of
government regulations on Italian wines limiting
various aspects of production, including the viticultural region, allowable grape varieties and
yields, minimum alcoholic strength, and often
aging requirements. DOC is no guarantee of a
wine's quality, only its authenticity. The categories, from the strictest to the least restrictive,
are:

> DOCG—Denominazione di Origine Controllata
> e Garantita;
>
> DOC—Denominazione di Origine Controllata;
>
> Vino Tipico—characteristic wine using grapes
> and production methods typical of the area;
>
> Vino da Tavola con indicazione geografica—
> table wine indicating location of viticultural
> region;
>
> Vino da Tavola—table wine. Again, no indica-
> tion of quality; some of Italy's poorest and
> some of its finest wines (such as those from
> nontraditional grape varieties) are in this
> category.

dolce–sweet.

frizzante–lightly sparkling.

riserva (speciale)—aged longer, frequently in cask,
than the minimum time required by DOC. The
wine must also have a higher level of alcohol.
Not an indication of quality, only of extra age
and higher alcohol.

rosato–rosé.

rosso–red.

rubino–ruby red.

secco–dry.

superiore–generally higher alcohol, sometimes having
longer age; does not mean superior.

Alcamo A light to medium-bodied, neu-
or Bianco tral, dry white, this is best
Alcamo drunk very young, while still
Sicily fresh. Goes well with fish, mixed
seafood.
Producers: Rapitalà, Fiume-
freddo

Bardolino A popular light-bodied, dry red,
Veneto often with a slight almond
character, Bardolino should be
served very young, lightly
chilled, with poultry, picnic
fare. With Valpolicella (red)
and Soave (white), it is one of
the most well-known, everyday
wines from the Veneto. A given
producer's Bardolino will be
lighter than his Valpolicella.
Producers: Masi, Bertani,
Guerrieri-Rizzardi

Bianchello This light, crisp, dry white is
del Metauro best drunk very young.
Marches **Producer:** Anzilotti-Solazzi

Bianco di A light, dry, fruity white, some-
Custoza what similar to Soave, this is
Veneto best when very young.
Producer: Gorgo (Roberto
Bricolo)

Chianti One of the largest wine-pro-
Tuscany ducing regions, Chianti boasts
literally hundreds of registered
vineyards and hundreds of producers making light to medium-
bodied, dry, somewhat firm red
wine broadly in two styles: Chianti and Chianti riserva. Chianti is a fresh and fruity wine
best drunk young (within 2 to
3 years) at a cool temperature.
This style is most often found
for under $5 and is sometimes

36

sold in the distinctive, straw-covered flasks (*fiaschi*). The riserva is a more serious style and is somewhat more expensive (See Chianti riserva, Wines $5–10). The best Chianti comes from the Classico zone; good Chianti is also produced in the Colli Fiorentini, Colli Senesi, and Rufina zones.

Producers: Cappelli, Riecine, Ruffino

Cortese
grape

Planted predominantly in northwestern Italy, this variety produces light, dry, firm white wines. They are most enjoyable drunk within 2 years of the vintage and with seafood or poultry. The best are from Gavi (See Gavi, Wines $5–10).

Producer (Region): Giustiniani (Oltrepò Pavese)

Est! Est!! Est!!!
di Montefiascone
Latium

A medium-bodied, soft, dry or off-dry white, this is best very young and with light pasta or poultry dishes.

Producer: Antinori

★ Favonio
Apulia

The estate of Attilio Simonini, produces very fine Pinot Bianco (see below), Chardonnay and a good Cabernet Franc (See Cabernet, Chardonnay, Wines $5–10).

Franciacorta
Pinot
Lombardy

These light-bodied, dry, fruity wines are among Italy's most interesting whites. They are best drunk within 2 years of the vintage, with freshwater fish, poultry.

Producer: Monti della Corte

Franciacorta Rosso
Lombardy

Medium-bodied, soft, dry reds, these have an herbaceous aroma and flavor. They are best within 2 to 4 years of the vintage.
Producers: Longhi- de Carli, Cattarich-Ducco

Gutturnio dei Colli Piacentini
Emilia-Romagna

These medium-bodied, vinous, dry or off-dry, tart and fruity reds sometimes display a cherrylike aroma. Drink at 2 to 4 years with braised meats, stews.
Producers: Kustermann, Mossi

Ischia Bianco
Campania

A medium-bodied, neutral dry white, Ischia Bianco is best drunk very young and very cold, with fish or seafood stew.
Producers: d'Ambra, Perrazzo

Lambrusco
grape

A variety grown in Emilia-Romagna, lambrusco grapes produce a generally fizzy, somewhat sweet, fruity red wine that alone accounts for over half the imports of Italian wine to the U.S. Most popular in the sweet *(amabile)* version, the best are dry and come from specific subvarieties of the lambrusco grape which give their names to the wines: Lambrusco di Sorbara, Grasparossa di Castelvetro, Reggiano, and Salamino di S. Croce. All Lambruscos should be consumed very young and chilled.
Producers: Contessa Matilde, Chiarli, Giacobazzi

★ **Lugana**
Lombardy

A light-bodied, fresh, and fruity white wine, fragrant, with a hint of almonds on the aroma, dry

or just off-dry, Lugana is similar to Soave. It is best when very young, and served with freshwater fish.
Producers: Visconti, Pietro Dal Cero, Fraccaroli, Ruffino

Malvasia di Casorzo d'Asti
Piedmont

Semisweet or sweet, lightly sparkling red wines, these are low in alcohol and grapey. Drink cold and very young, with fresh fruit or slightly sweet cakes.

Malvasia di Castelnuovo Don Bosco
Piedmont

This sparkling red is similar to the Malvasia di Casorzo d'Asti, above.
Producer: Balbiano

Malvasia di Ziano
Emilia-Romagna

Fizzy, dryish or lightly sweet, this Malvasia is a white wine with an aroma and flavor reminiscent of apples. Best drunk very young.
Producers: Mossi, Kustermann

Merlot
grape

Mostly planted in northeastern Italy, the variety produces red wines similar to those from the cabernet grape (See Wines $5–10), though softer and smoother. They have an herbaceous, sometimes grassy, character, and are best drunk within 1 to 3 years, rarely past 4. Italian merlot is sometimes blended with cabernet, as in French Bordeaux wines.
Producers (Regions): Hofstätter (Alto Adige); Lazzarini "Campo del Lago" (Colli Berici); Formentini, Russiz Superiore (Collio); Pighin (Grave del Friuli)

★ **Montecarlo**
Tuscany
A medium-bodied, smooth, dry white wine, Montecarlo is best when young, at 1 to 2 years, with poultry or veal. It is among Italy's better whites.
Producers: Buonamico, Teso

Montepulciano d'Abruzzo
Abruzzo
Generally medium-bodied fruity, soft, dry reds, occasionally they are full-bodied and robust. They are best drunk within 2 to 3 years of age, but can stand 4 years.
Producers: Rosso della Quercia, Duchi di Castelluccio, Tollo

Pinot Bianco
grape
Planted throughout Italy, particularly in Lombardy and the northeastern regions, pinot bianco grapes produce light to medium-bodied, dry, fruity white wines that are sometimes crisp, other times round and smooth. Zones to look for are Alto Adige, Colli Orientali del Friuli, Collio, Oltrepò Pavese, and Trentino. The wines are best within 2 years, occasionally longer. Drink with seafood, poultry, or veal. (See Pinot Bianco, Wines $5–10.)
Producers (Regions): Favonio (Apulia); Pighin (Grave del Friuli); Fini (Valdadige); Lagariavini (Trentino)

Regaleali
Sicily
This is a brand name for white and red wines, medium-bodied and dry. The white is best drunk very young; the red ages to about 4 or 5 years.

Rosso Cònero
Marches

A medium-bodied, soft, fruity, dry red wine, this is good from 1–3 years of age but will last to 4, rarely more. Serve lightly chilled with white meat or poultry.

Rosso Piceno
Marches

A similar red to Rosso Cònero, Rosso Piceno is generally a little better. It is best drunk before 5 years of age.
Producers: La Torraccia, Vallone

Sangiovese di Romagna
Emilia-Romagna

Some of the best varietally-labelled Sangiovese wines come from this zone. They should be drunk between 2 and 4 years of the vintage.
Producer: Pasolini

Soave
Veneto

A light, dry, fruity white wine, with an almond-like aroma and a slightly bitter aftertaste, Soave is best drunk as young as possible. It is good with seafood.
Producers: Pieropan, Visconti, Masi, Bertani, Bolla

★ **Spanna**
grape
80, <u>79</u>, <u>78</u>, <u>74</u>, <u>70</u>

Another name for the nebbiolo grape (See Nebbiolo, Wines $5–10) grown in the northwest. Wines sold under the label Spanna are medium-bodied, fruity, firm, dry reds with a characteristic flowery aroma that has a tarlike component. Most should be drunk within 3 to 4 years; the best of them can be aged up to 30.
Producers: Barra, Nervi, Antoniolo

Tocai
grape

Planted mostly in the north-east and Lombardy, tocai produces light to medium-bodied, fruity and dry white wines occasionally with an almond-like note and a faint bitterness. They are best drunk within 1 year, at most 2, of the vintage, with fish, poultry, or pasta. Collio and Colli Orientali del Fruili are the zones to look for. **Producers (Region):** Doro Princic, Russiz Superiore (Collio)

★ **Torre Quarto**
Apulia
79, 77, 75, 74, 73, 71

This single-estate wine is a true bargain at the price. Medium to full-bodied, flavorful, dry red, it ages quite well and should be drunk from 4 to 5 years of vintage.

Valpolicella
Veneto

This well-known, light, fruity, dry red wine from the Veneto is somewhat fuller than a Bardolino (for a given producer). It is quite agreeable when young, within 4 years. Serve chilled.
Producers: Allegrini, Le Ragose, Quintarelli, Tedeschi, Masi, Tommasi, Bolla

WINES $5–10

★ **Aglianico del Vulture**
Basilicata
79, 77, 73

This full-bodied, robust, red wine has a slight aroma of cherries. Drink from 6 years of vintage.
Producer: D'Angelo

Albana di Romagna
Emilia-Romagna

Medium-bodied, dry (*secco*) or lightly sweet (*amabile*), white wine, sometimes with an aroma

suggesting pears, Albana di Romagna is best drunk within 1 or 2 years, not past 3. The dry style accompanies seafood, poultry, or veal well; drink the lightly sweet wine with pasta or poultry in cream sauce.
Producers: Fattoria Paradiso, Pasolini, Vallunga

Barbera
grape

This is a prolific variety in the northwest, especially Piedmont, and some other regions including Emilia-Romagna and Lombardy. Its wines are medium to full-bodied, fruity, tart, dry reds, with cherries on the aroma, and are best drunk from 1 to 4 years of the vintage.

Barbera d'Alba
Piedmont
81, 79, 78

A hearty Barbera, this comes from one of the two best growing zones (the other being Asti). Drink within 4 years; some will live for 5 or 6.
Producers: Vietti, Gaja, Ceretto, Pio Cesare

Barbera d'Asti
Piedmont
81, 79, 78

A fruitier, softer Barbera than those of Alba, this is good within 4 years, and may live to 5 or 6.
Producers: Contratto, Duca d'Asti

Cabernet
grape

By itself on a label, "Cabernet" can mean the wine is made from cabernet franc or cabernet sauvignon grapes or a combination of the two. Both varieties are mostly grown in the northeast, where they produce medium-bodied, soft, dry, somewhat herbaceous, fruity red wines, sometimes with a bell pepper character to the aroma and flavor. The wines are similar to Merlots, but somewhat firmer and fuller, and generally best from 2 to 4 years of the vintage; a few age well.

Producers (Regions): Lazzarini "Le Rive Rosse" (Colli Berici); Tadei "Villa Belvedere" (Colli Orientali del Friuli); Formentini, Gradnik, Russiz Superiore (Collio); Pighin (Grave del Friuli); Venegazzù (Montello e Colli Asolani); Lagariavini, Fini (Trentino); Favonio (Apulia), See Wines Under $5.

★ Cabernet dell'Alto Adige
Trentino-Alto Adige
79, <u>78</u>, <u>75</u>

These are definitely the Cabernets to look for. The best from the Alto Adige are the finest produced in Italy and can age over a decade.

Producer: Herrnhofer

Carema
Piedmont
79, 78, <u>74</u>, <u>70</u>

Medium-bodied and firm, these dry red wines have an aroma of flowers and fruit. Best at 5 to 10 years, they can live longer.

Producers: Produttori dei "Nebbiolo di Carema", Luigi Ferrando

Carmignano
Tuscany
79, 78, <u>77</u>, <u>75</u>, <u>73</u>, <u>71</u>

A dry, medium-bodied, red wine with some refinement, Carmignano is similar to Chianti riserva, but more consistent in quality. It is best from 3 to 4 years until 10 or 12 years from vintage.

Producers: Villa Capezzana, Fattoria Il Poggiolo

Chardonnay or Pinot Chardonnay grape Mostly northern plantings, the chardonnay produces dry white wines, sometimes crisp, sometimes soft and fruity. Similar to a Pinot Bianco wine from the same producer, a chardonnay wine will be fuller-bodied with more character. Best drunk within 1 to 2 or perhaps 3 years, with fish, poultry, or veal.
Producers: Eno Friulia, Pojer & Sandri, Favonio, Lagaria, Bollini

Chianti riserva Tuscany 79, 78, <u>77</u>, <u>75</u>, <u>71</u>, <u>70</u> A fuller and firmer style of Chianti, the riserva can be drunk from 5 or 6 years to about 10 or 13 years from vintage; riservas from some producers can live for two or three decades. The best are aristocratic, but overall the quality is variable, and you should select cautiously by producer and vintage. The best are from the Classico zone; other fine riservas are produced in Rufina and Colli Fiorentini. They accompany lamb or beef.
Producers (Regions): Monsanto, Le Bocce, Villa Colombaio, Cappelli "Montagliari e Castellnuzza", Villa Antinori, Castello di Uzzano, Ruffino Riserva Ducale (especially the Gold Label), Badia a Coltibuono (Classico); Castello di Nipozzano, Selvapiana (Rufina); Tenuta Capezzana (Montalbano)

Corvo Sicily This is the brand name for a medium-bodied, dry, fruity white wine which should be drunk very young. Serve with seafood or poultry.

Dolcetto Mostly grown in Piedmont, dol-
grape cetto grapes produce medium-bodied, fruity, dry red wines, which are Italy's answer to Beaujolais, although somewhat fuller and more serious. The wine can be charming when young; drink slightly chilled at 1 or 2 years, up to 4 years. It goes well with pasta, salami, picnic fare. Look for bottles from the Alba zone; Diano d'Alba and Ovada zones also produce fine Dolcetto.
Producers (Regions): Vietti, Bruno Giacosa, Gaja, Terre del Barolo (Alba); Terre del Barolo (Diano d'Alba)

Gattinara At its rare best, Gattinara is a
Piedmont dry, firm, aristocratic red wine,
79, 78, <u>74</u>, <u>70</u> among the finest from Italy. Like many nebbiolo-based wines, it has a bouquet suggesting flowers, and a firm, tannic backbone. Good after 6 years, the best can live for a decade or two.
Producers: Monsecco, Nervi, Barra

Gavi A light, dry, often crisp white
Piedmont wine; this is one of Italy's better whites and is best when young.
Producers: La Scolca (especially Gavi di Gavi), La Battistina, La Giustiniana, Contratto

46

Ghemme
Piedmont
79, 78, <u>76</u>, <u>74</u>

A medium-bodied, dry red, Ghemme is similar to Gattinara without attaining the heights but more consistent in quality. Good from 5 to 7 years, it can last a decade.
Producer: Ponti

Grignolino
grape

A variety grown mostly in Piedmont, it produces light, dry, fruity, often pale-colored red wines with a fragrant aroma. The wine is best within 2 years. Serve lightly chilled, with pork, poultry, picnic fare.
Producers: Vietti, Bruno Giacosa, Nuova Cappelletta

Grumello
Lombardy
79, 78, <u>74</u>

A medium-bodied, dry red, Grumello is good with 4 to 8 years of aging, although it can last longer. It is one of the four wines from the Valtellina Superiore zone (see below).
Producers: San Carlo, Nera, Rainoldi, Nino Negri

Inferno
Lombardy
<u>79</u>, <u>78</u>, <u>74</u>

A medium-bodied, dry red, drinkable from 3 to 6 years of age and longer, Inferno is from the Valtellina Superiore zone (see below).
Producers: San Carlo, Rainoldi, Nera, Nino Negri

Lacryma Christi
Campania

The Lacryma Christi are red, white, and rosé wines in a range of styles from dry to semisweet, still and sparkling, with normal alcohol or fortified. Of these, the still, dry, regular alcohol red and white are most commonly found and the best. Drink the red 3 to 6 years old,

with meat or poultry in piquant sauces; the white, drink very young with fish in stews or tomato-based sauces.
Producer: Mastroberardino

★ **Lagrein dell'Alto Adige**
Trentino-Alto Adige
79, 78, <u>75</u>, <u>74</u>

A medium-bodied, dry red with a slightly herbaceous character, this wine is often similar to cabernet or merlot-based wines. Drink from 4 to 10 years of age.
Producer: Herrnhofer

Malvasia
grape

Popular variety grown throughout Italy, malvasia produces a wide range of red and white wines. In central Italy it is often blended with trebbiano; it is more frequently vinified alone in the south and on the islands, where it generally produces amber-colored, semisweet to sweet, full-bodied wines, high or moderately high in alcohol. Malvasias age moderately well. (See also Malvasia, Wines Under $5).

Malvasia delle Lipari
Sicily

Without question this is Italy's best Malvasia. It is amber-colored wine with an aroma of almonds and flowers, some sweetness, and a high degree of alcohol. Drink between 3 to 6 years of the vintage.
Producer: Lo Schiavo

Mori Vecio
Trentino-Alto Adige

A cabernet-merlot blend from Lagaria, this medium-bodied, firm, dry red wine has an herbaceous character and a tarlike, occasionally floral aroma. At its best from 5 to 8 years, it can last a decade.

Müller-Thurgau
grape

A variety planted predominantly in Trentino-Alto Adige and, to a lesser extent, in Friuli-Venezia Giulia, müller-thurgau produces light, dry, fruity whites that are best when young and fresh, within 1 or 2 years of the vintage.
Producers: Pojer & Sandri, Lagaria

Nebbiolo
grape

This variety (also known as spanna; See Wines Under $5) is planted mostly in northwestern Italy, where it yields medium to full-bodied, dry reds, some of Italy's finest and most aristocratic wines. When labelled Nebbiolo, followed by a place name, it is good everyday wine; those above $5 offer the most interest.
Producers: Gaja, Aldo Conterno, di Gresy

Nebbiolo
d'Alba
Piedmont
81, 80, 79, 78

Alba is generally considered the best zone for Nebbiolo, but it is usually surpassed by the Nebbiolos of the Barolo and Barbaresco zones, often sold as vino da tavola, or Nebbiolo del Piemonte without DOC recognition.
Producers: Vietti, Bruno Giacosa, Mascarello

Orvieto
Umbria

A light to medium-bodied, dry or off-dry, pale white wine, Orvieto can be fruity but more often is neutral. Best drunk as young as possible, within the year, it is rarely good past 2 years. Serve with mixed seafood or pasta in light sauce.
Producers: La Velette, Vaselli, Antinori

ÿ

Pinot Bianco
grape

The Pinot Bianco wines in this price range are similar to the wines under $5, but from selected producers they are more distinguished.
Producers (Regions): Herrnhofer (Alto Adige); Russiz Superiore, Formentini (Collio); Fontanafredda (Piedmont); Zeni (Trentino)

Pinot Grigio
grape

Planted mostly in the northeast and Lombardy, this variety produces light to medium-bodied, dry, sometimes firm, fruity white wines often with a pear-like aroma. Drink within 1–2 years of the vintage, with simple veal or poultry dishes. When a Pinot Grigio is more expensive than a Pinot Bianco wine from a given producer, as is often the case, buy the Pinot Bianco.
Producers (Regions): Herrnhofer (Alto Adige); Russiz Superiore (Collio); Eno Friulia (della Venezia); Pighin (Grave del Friuli); Lagariavini (Trentino); Fini, Rotalvini (Valdadige)

Pinot Nero
grape

Generally, this variety produces medium-bodied, fruity, dry reds in the northeast and Lombardy, with mixed results, but it is most successful in sparkling wines. At its best, wines from pinot nero have an aroma and flavor reminiscent of strawberries. Drink young, perhaps within 3 or 4 years.
Producer (Region): Lazzarini "Rosso del Rocolo" (Colli Berici)

Pomino Bianco
Tuscany

A medium-bodied, dry white wine with some character, it is made from mostly pinot bianco grapes. Drink within 2 to 3 years.
Producer: Frescobaldi

Primitivo di Manduria
Apulia

A full-bodied, robust, inky red, this wine is generally fruity, slightly sweet, and high in alcohol. Drink from about 4 to 6 years, although it can last a little longer.
Producer: Amanda

Riesling Renano
grape

Also known as Rheinriesling, this grape is mostly planted in the northeast. Its best wines are light-bodied, dry and well-balanced, distinguished whites with a delicate floral perfume. Best drunk young.
Producers (Regions): Herrnhofer, J. Hofstätter; (Alto Adige); Eno Friulia (delle Venezia)

Rosso dei Vigneti di Brunello
Tuscany
79, 78, 77

A medium-bodied, dry, flavorful red, the wine bears some resemblance to its more expensive relative, Brunello di Montalcino (which is made from older vines and aged longer). Drink between about 3 to 5 years of the vintage.
Producers: Altesino, Caparzo

Rosso di Sava

See Primitivo di Manduria, above.

Rosso Toscano di Brunello

See Rosso dei Vigneti di Brunello, above.

★ Rubesco
Umbria
79, 78,
<u>77</u>, <u>75</u>, <u>74</u>, <u>73</u>, <u>71</u>, <u>70</u>

A medium-bodied, dry, flavorful red wine, Rubesco is smooth in texture and ages well. Similar to Chianti but more reliable, it is good from 4 to 8 years and can live longer.
Producer: Lungarotti

Sassella
Lombardy
79, <u>78</u>, <u>74</u>

A medium-bodied, firm, dry red, Sassella is often considered the best of the four Valtellina Superiore wines (see below). Drink from 5 to 8 years.
Producers: San Carlo, Nera, Rainoldi, Nino Negri

Sauvignon
grape

Most plantings are in the northeast, producing wines light to medium in body, dry and white, sometimes with a green herbaceous character. Drink young, within 1 or 2 years.
Producers: Borgo Conventi, Russiz Superiore

Teroldego Rotaliano
Trentino-Alto Adige
80, <u>77</u>, <u>75</u>, <u>74</u>

A medium-bodied, fruity dry red, often among the best reds of Trentino, this wine sometimes has an herbaceous character similar to a Merlot or Cabernet. It is good with 2 to 5 years of age and can last longer. Drink with steak or chops.
Producers: Barone de Cles, Zeni, Lagaria

Torgiano

See Rubesco, above; Rubesco Riserva, Wines $10–15; Torre di Giano, below.

Torre di Giano
Umbria

This is a medium-bodied, fruity, dry white wine; the riserva is fuller and less flavorful. Both are best when young; drink with veal or poultry dishes.
Producer: Lungarotti

Valgella
Lombardy
<u>79</u>, <u>78</u>, <u>74</u>

The lightest and fastest-maturing of the dry red Valtellina Superiore wines (See below). Generally best from 3 to 5 years of age, it can last longer.

Producers: San Carlo, Rainoldi, Nera

Valtellina Superiore
Lombardy

Medium-bodied, dry, fruity red wines often with a vaguely nut-like aroma. Among the lightest of the nebbiolo-based wines, they range in body from Valgella (the lightest), through Inferno, Grumello, and Sassella (the fullest). See individual entries, above.

Venegazzù
Veneto

A single estate, Venegazzù produces some good dry red cabernets and other quality wines, in particular the aristo-cratic Venegazzù Riserva della Casa, black label (See Wines $10–15).

Verdicchio
grape

Mostly planted in Marches, this variety produces light-bodied, dry, crisp white wines. Drink under 2 years, with seafood of all types.

Verdicchio dei Castelli di Jesi
Marches

This is the most famous wine, of the Verdicchio zone that is regularly imported to the United States.

Producers: Garofoli, Ronchi, Fazi-Battaglia

Vino Nobile di A glorified Chianti Classico
Montepulciano riserva, this is often overpriced
Tuscany for its quality. The best, which
79, 78, 77, 75 can be very fine, are very rare,
and you should select carefully
from recommended producers
and by vintage. Medium-bodied,
red, firm, dry, it is best from 5
to 8 years of the vintage, rarely
older.
Producers: Dal Cerro, Boscar-
elli, Fanetti, Melini

WINES $10–15

Amarone This is an intense, full-flavored,
Veneto hearty red with high alcohol,
79, 77, 74, 71 an almond-like aroma, and a
bitter almond aftertaste. Good
after a full 6 years, it can age a
decade or two.
Producers: Allegrini, Quintarelli, Le Ragose, Masi, Bertani, Bolla, Tedeschi, Tommasi

Barbaresco A full-bodied, dry red, this wine
Piedmont is similar to Barolo but some-
79, 78, 74, 71, 70 what softer, smoother, and
faster-maturing. It is drinkable
from 6 to 8 years; the best vintages age very well. Serve with
game.
Producers: Produttori del
Barbaresco, Gaja, Bruno Giacosa, Moresco, Bricco Asili,
Ceretto, Vietti, di Gresy, La
Spinona, Castello di Neive,
Glicine

Barolo
Piedmont
79, 78, <u>74</u>, 71, <u>70</u>

A full-bodied, aristocratic wine, it ages very well and is one of the most famous Italian reds. It needs at least 8 years aging; serve with game or roast red meat.
Producers: Vietti, Bruno Giacosa, Aldo Conterno, Cogno-Marcarini, Ceretto, Mascarello, Ratti, Barale, Contratto

Le Pergole Torte
Tuscany
78, 77

The medium-bodied, firm, well-balanced, dry red has overtones of new oak (it is aged in small barrels) and is a single vineyard wine. It is ready from its sixth year. Drink with lamb, beef.

Rubesco Riserva
Umbria
78, 77, 75, <u>74</u>, <u>71</u>, <u>70</u>

A full, distinguished Rubesco, the riserva is medium-bodied, dry, balanced and flavorful, with a rich, deep aroma and a smooth, even velvety texture. Reliable. It ages very well; drink after 7 to 8 years.
Producer: Lungarotti

Taurasi
Campania
79, 77, <u>73</u>, <u>71</u>

A medium to full-bodied, aristocratic, dry red, Taurasi often has an aroma recalling cherries. It ages very well, up to 25 years or more; drink after 7 to 8 years, with roast meat, game. It is among the most reliable of Italy's better wines.
Producer: Mastroberardino

Venegazzù Riserva della Casa
Veneto
79, 78

This aristocratic, medium-bodied, dry red is from cabernet sauvignon and other grape varieties. Good with 6 to 8 years aging, it can live a decade. Serve with steak, roasts, lamb. Select the black over the white label.

Brunello di Montalcino
Tuscany
79, 78, 77, 75, <u>71</u>, 70

A full-bodied, dry red wine, this is somewhat astringent when young, becoming smooth and velvety in texture with age. At its best, though it is rare, an aristocratic wine. Best after 8 years, it can be very long-lived. **Producers:** Fattoria dei Barbi (Colombini), Emilio Costanti, Tenuta Il Poggione, Altesino, Lisini, Col d'Orcia, Caparzo

Picolit
Friuli-Venezia Giulia

This medium-bodied, sweet white wine comes from the extremely shy-bearing picolit grape. The best are a special treat, with a floral, slightly pear-like aroma, smooth texture, and complex flavor. Expensive and rarely worth the price, it is best within 2 or 3 years of the vintage.

San Giorgio
Umbria

A medium-bodied, distinguished, dry red, this wine is rich in flavor, with complex overtones. First produced in 1977 by Dott. Lungarotti, it should age very well.

Sassicaia
Tuscany
79, 78, 77, <u>75</u>

A medium-bodied, well-balanced, dry red, sometimes aristocratic, it is a single-estate wine, produced primarily from cabernet sauvignon. Drink from 7 to 10 years of the vintage.

Tignanello
Tuscany
78, <u>77</u>, <u>75</u>, <u>71</u>

A medium-bodied, well-balanced, aristocratic dry red, this wine has a somewhat herbaceous character from the small amount of cabernet sauvignon in the predominantly sangiovese blend.

THE WINES OF Germany

The wines of Germany are unique as even the least exalted bottle reveals. This is partly a result of grape variety (principally the riesling), soil quality, and tradition, but it is mostly climate.

The vineyards of Germany are the most northerly of all the world's wine-growing regions, on a latitude equivalent to that of Nova Scotia. The grapes would not ripen at all this far north but for the kindly breezes of the Gulf Stream, which blow from the south and west through the Rhineland. Even so, it is a harsh climate for grape growing, with summers which are not long and seldom very hot. So it is the Autumn which makes or breaks a vintage. If it is balmy into October, if the first frosts hold off long enough, the growers of Germany will make wines that will be remembered for years.

Such years occur perhaps three times each decade, with most vintages being hampered by insufficient warmth. But with an inventiveness amounting to genius, the Germans have turned a capricious climate to their advantage, making delicate, low-alcohol wines which are the envy and wonder of winemakers all over the world. No other white wine has the delicacy of a German wine; none other attains such perfume and such a balance of sweetness and acidity.

Most white wines are a harmony between fruit, alcohol, and wood. Alcohol and extract combine to form what we call body in a white wine. Body provides the background on which nuances of fruit and wood are tasted.

It is all different in Germany. Grapes ripen slowly in the pale northern sun. The resultant wines have very little alcohol, but the grapes develop a vivid flavor and fragrance which could never be achieved by quick, easy ripening.

The first thing you will notice is the astonishing perfume of a German wine. As you drink the wine, you will notice its lightness, delicacy of structure, and extraordinary clarity, all supported by an uncanny balance of sweetness and acidity which prevents the wine from tasting either too sugary or too tart.

The German wines are predominantly white, with some light reds for local consumption, but few merit export. Occasionally you might see a Spätburgunder (Pinot Noir) wine for sale; try it as a curiosity, and drink it as you would a light Beaujolais.

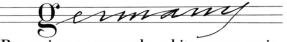

Pre-eminent among the white grape varieties is the riesling, the great grape of Germany, often grown elsewhere but never with the same success. These late ripening, small berries yield wines of great elegance and harmony.

There are three other important varieties: the silvaner, a plump, juicy grape giving a rather flat, tangy wine with a grassy flavor; it is usually blended into Liebfraumilch. The müller-thurgau is an early ripening grape giving plausibly attractive wine with a musky tone and low acidity; it is another staple of most blends, including Liebfraumilch. Gewürztraminer, the famous, spicy grape of Alsace, gives a looser-knit, sweet wine in Germany.

READING THE LABEL

Understanding the label on a bottle of German wine is far less difficult than it at first appears. Part of the difficulty is that the regulations governing wine labeling in Germany are very precise, and sometimes there is almost too much information.

The first word on the label is usually the name of the village or district *(bereich)*, ending in *-er*, where the wine was produced. Exceptions are those few vineyards which are so famous that their name can stand alone, such as Schloss Vollrads or Steinberger. Next comes a more specific name of the vineyard *(einzellage)* in the case of better wines, or a general collection of vineyards *(grosslage)*. Generally, but not always, this is followed by the name of the grape; for better wines this will almost always be riesling (in much of the Mosel, nothing else is grown so the name is often omitted). Finally, there is the quality level of the wine.

German wines are classified by the ripeness of the grapes. Varying degrees of ripeness produce wines of varying characters.

The level known as *Qualitätswein* (or QbA) designates a wine made from generally unripe grapes. The wines are *chaptalized* (have sugar added during fermentation) to bring them up to the required alcoholic strength. They should be drunk within two years of vintage date, and are usually innocuous, light, and thirst-quenching wines, with some character and an attractive fruitiness. Be careful to buy only recommended bottles; bad QbA wines are coarse and unbalanced.

Riper grapes may produce *Qualitätswein mit Prädikat* (QmP), quality wine with distinction. This category is subdivided into ascending levels of ripeness and methods of harvest.

Kabinett, the first, is made from ripe grapes picked during the normal harvest ("normal" being a highly relative term in Germany, where the harvest is only just underway in October, by which time most French grapes are already in the vats fermenting). Kabinett wines are light but

full of finesse and purity of flavor. There is real quality here. Usually they are the driest of the QmPs, and are always the most delicate of all German wines. Drink within two to four years, although well-stored bottles may live longer.

Spätlese, the second level, is made from late-harvested grapes which are fully ripe but not overripe. A longer time on the vine gives a richer, rounder wine, with greater depth of flavor than a Kabinett, and usually a little more sweetness. Generally, a Spätlese is best between three to seven years old although excellent vintages may continue developing for fifteen years.

Auslese wines are made from specially selected bunches of grapes from which all unripe or unhealthy berries are removed. The wine is dazzlingly aromatic with a marked increase in lushness and intensity of fruit that reaches its peak in five to ten years, and may live for twenty-five years. It is usually sweet enough to serve as a dessert wine or even as an aperitif, in the French manner.

Beerenauslese wines are painstakingly made by an individual, berry-by-berry selection of overripe grapes, or grapes which have been attacked by noble rot (a highly beneficial fungus which sucks the water out of ripe grapes, concentrating their acids and sugars in the process). These wines can only be made in the tiniest quantities, as the shrivelled grapes contain perhaps a single healthy drop of syrupy juice. But what a wine they create! Fiercely concentrated with a whole kaleidoscope of flavors and a natural honeyed sweetness, the best are breathtakingly lovely and fit for the finest occasions.

Trockenbeerenauslese is essentially the same as Beerenauslese, except that the degree of overripeness is even higher. In fact these grapes are nearly raisins by the time the noble rot is through with them. Once harvested (and a single picker in a full day's work might collect enough grapes for one bottle of wine), the juice is so exceptionally rich it is fiendishly difficult to ferment. There are hardly words to describe the wine—its staggering opulence, and sheer gorgeousness of flavor.

Last of the QmPs, *Eiswein* is a sweet wine made from frozen grapes of exceptionally firm acidity and a remarkable piquant sweetness. Until 1982 you could see Eiswein in conjunction with another Prädikat (for example, Dhron Hofberger Auslese Eiswein), but now all Eiswein must attain the ripeness of a Beerenauslese, and the word *Eiswein* exists as a quality level of its own. *Riesling Beerenauslese, Trockenbeerenauslese,* and *Eiswein* begin to reach maturity at about ten years old, often living fifty to seventy-five years.

Beginning in 1982, there is a new category of simple wine called *Landwein,* or country wine. The law insists these wines

be dry or semidry. They will be light and cheap, but better dry wines can be had from other sources. Dry German wines (designated by the word *Trocken*) are to be avoided.

In most cases, the label will also carry a vintage date, and in all cases it will carry the alcoholic strength, expressed in percentage by volume, and the name of the shipper.

If a wine is a QbA or QmP, it must carry an official approval number (AP number) which shows it has passed the government board after analysis and testing. It is this thorough control that protects the consumer of German wine, for the tasting board ensures that the wine meets all the requirements for a wine of that type from that region before it can be accepted. This kind of rigorous testing makes winemaking in other parts of the world seem almost haphazard. But it does mean that when you buy a Kabinett or a Spatlëse from a given region you can be sure that you will be getting a certain type of wine. If the tasting panel does not approve a wine, it may award it a lower quality designation, approve it as an Auslese instead of a Beerenauslese, for example.

Because the grapes are individually picked, in a good year a vineyard may submit a whole range of wines, from a Trockenbeerenauslese downward. In a poor year, it may only make one or two wines, as only its ripest grapes can make a Kabinett wine. Because of this, and because a single district will have several different vineyards, each with several different owners controlling a small piece of the vineyard, it is particularly difficult to make general recommendations about German wines. The listing that follows is a selection of good, generally available German wines. German law guarantees that you will be getting the wine described on the label, so refer back to the relevant region and QbA or QmP category for tasting notes.

GLOSSARY OF TERMS

abfüller–bottler.

anaugebiete (gebiet)–wine region. Eleven are designated by German law.

A.P.–approval number for QbA and QmP wines.

aus eigenem lesegut–estate bottled.

edelfäule–noble rot, the mold *botrytis cinerea* that penetrates grape skins, concentrating sugars and flavors.

eiswein–literally "ice wine." Rare, sweet wine made usually when the grapes are frozen on the vine and pressed while still frozen. Can occur as late as January or February after harvest.

halbtrocken–half dry.

keller–cellar.

lieblich–used for slightly sweet wines.

Qualitätswein bestimmter Anbaugebiete (QbA)–

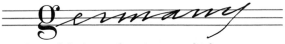

wines of designated regions to which sugar may be added (before fermentation) when grapes do not fully ripen.

Qualitätswein mit Prädikat (QmP)–quality wine with distinction. Includes the top 5 levels of German wines, made only in years when the grapes ripen fully. No sugar is added. In ascending order of quality and natural sweetness they are:

> *Kabinett*–the most delicate and driest of the QmP wines.

> *Spätlese*–late-picked, from grapes left on the vine to ripen further. Wines are richer and rounder than Kabinett.

> *Auslese*–late-picked, selected bunches of grapes, affected by *botrytis cinerea* (see *edelfäule*). Auslese and the next two QmPs are only made in good years.

> *Beerenauslese* (BA)–late-ripened selected berries. Only those attacked by *botrytis* are used to produce small quantities of luscious sweet wines.

> *Trockenbeerenauslese* (TBA)–selected dried berries, almost raisins, when harvested. Botrytised grapes left to dry until the sugars concentrate, and can produce incredibly rich, sweet wines.

süss–sweet.

tafelwein–table wine; lowest classification of wines. Ranked below QbA.

trocken–dry.

weinhändler–wine merchant or shipper.

weingut–vineyard property or domain.

weingutsbesitzer–the owner of the vineyard property.

weinkellerei–wineceller, winery.

THE GROWING REGIONS

There are eleven regions of Germany. The first five are the most significant for the consumer in the United States.

Rheingau: home of the finest Rieslings, aristocratic, compact, and splendidly flavored.

Rheinhessen: produces soft, easy-to-drink wines, with a few very fine Rieslings from the Nierstein area.

Rheinpfalz: spicy, earthy wines, with suave, elegant Rieslings from the best sites.

Mosel-Saar-Ruwer: lissome, stony, racy wines, lighter and more feminine than Rhine wines. A good Mosel expresses the fruit of pears and apples, while a Rhine suggests peaches and apricots.

Nahe: similar to Rheingaus. Lighter and more flowery. Some show the crisp, grapey bite of Ruwer wines.

Franken: muscular, very earthy wines, mostly dry and quite unlike any other German wines. Sold in flagonlike bottles, and rarely exported.

Baden: large, disjointed district; the best wines are warm and spicy, others are merely heavy.

Württemberg: pithy, steely wines, with some taut, assertive Rieslings from the better sites.

Mittelrhein: mostly tart wines, but hot summers produce memorable Rieslings.

Hessisches Bergstrasse: good, fleshy Rieslings which seldom leave their region.

Ahr: light, quaffable reds and extremely delicate whites are all drunk locally.

Ayler Kupp Riesling Kabinett 1982, Winzerverein Ayl, Saar

★ **Bereich Bernkastel, "Green Label," Riesling,** Deinhard, Mosel

★ **Black Forest Girl Zentralkellerei,** Badisches Winzergenossenschaften Breisach, Baden

Dürkheimer Spielberg Riesling Kabinett 1981, Winzergenossenschaft Vier Jahreszeiten, Rheinphalz

Erbacher Steinmorgen Riesling Kabinett 1981, Winzergenossenschaft Erbach, Rheingau

Liebfraumilch "Little Rhine Bear", Winzergenossenschaft, Rheinhessen

Niersteiner Auflangen Riesling Kabinett 1982, "von Lersner" (von Plettenberg is the bottler), Rheinhessen

★ **Oestricher Klosterberg Riesling QbA 1982,** Wittemann, Rheingau

Riesling Bürklin-Wolf, (Schoonmacher selections), Rheinphalz

Riesling von Kesselstatt (Schoonmacher selections), Mosel

Schlossböckelheimer Kupfergrube Riesling QbA 1982, von Plettenberg, Nahe

WINES $5–10

Geisenheimer Rothenberg Riesling Kabinett 1981, Deinhard, Rheingau

Hattenheimer Nussbrunnen Riesling Kabinett 1981, von Simmern, Rheingau

Hochheimer Hölle Riesling Kabinett 1980, Schloss Schönborn, Rheingau

★ **Kiedricher Gräfenberg Riesling Kabinett 1979,** Groenesteyn, Rheingau

Niersteiner Kranzberg Riesling Kabinett 1981, Franz Karl Schmitt, Rheinhessen

Schlossböckelheimer Felsenberg Riesling Spätlese 1979, Crusius (Deinhard), Nahe

Uerziger Würzgarten Riesling Kabinett 1981, von Beeres, Mosel

★ **Wachenheimer Mandelgarten Riesling Spätlese 1981,** Bürklin-Wolf, Rheinphalz

WINES $10–15

Avelsbacher Hammerstein Riesling Auslese 1976, Staatsweingüter, Mosel

Eitelsbacher Karthäuserhofberger Burgberg Riesling Auslese 1976, Tyrell, Mosel

Forster Ungeheuer Riesling Auslese 1976, Basserman Jordan, Rheinphalz

★ **Hochheimer Domdechaney Riesling Auslese 1976,** Domdechant Werner, Rheingau

Keidricher Sandgrub Riesling Auslese 1976, Groenesteyn, Rheingau

Niersteiner Hipping Riesling Auslese 1976, Franz Karl Schmitt, Rheinhessen

Steinberger Riesling Spätlese 1976, Staatsweingüter, Rheingau

WINES OVER $15

★ **Dhron Hofberger Riesling Auslese 1976,** Bishöfliches Priesterseminar, Mosel

★ **Hattenheimer Wisselbrunnen Riesling Auslese 1976,** Schloss Reinhartshausen, Rheingau

Maximin Grünhäuser Abstberg Riesling Auslese Nr. 46 1976, Grünhaus, Mosel

Rauenthaler Baiken Riesling Auslese 1976, Schloss Eltz, Rheingau

Scharzhofberger Riesling Auslese 1976, Egon Müller, Mosel

★ **Winkeler Hasensprung Riesling Auslese 1976,** Landgraf von Hessen, Rheingau

THE WINES OF Spain & PORTUGAL

*A*lthough produced almost next door to each other, the best wines of Spain and Portugal share very few characteristics. Of course, each country has always been known for its acclaimed fortified wines, Sherry and Port, and both countries are also known for enormous bulk exports of inexpensive wine to France and northern Europe, for simple "carafe" consumption or for blending. But these broad similarities aside, Spain and Portugal part ways—each has distinguished table wines of its own.

In the past, the best wines from Spain and Portugal were well-kept secrets (extraordinary wines at excellent prices), but judging from recent export figures, American wine lovers have discovered the grand wines of the Iberian peninsula. Some connoisseurs have even declared that Spanish red wines are the only reds in the world (besides a few from California) that can rival Bordeaux and Burgundy in excellence— and for a fraction of the price. For example, in the 1979 Wine Olympics organized by the well-known French food and wine publishers, Gault and Millau, a Spanish red— Torres Gran Coronas, Black Label— won first prize in a blind tasting of 330 wines. It costs about seven dollars a bottle. Château Latour came in second—at about five times the price.

SPAIN

Spain has the largest area of land planted in vine of any country in Europe. It is, however, only the third largest producer of wine, after Italy and France, mostly the result of Spain's attachment to tradition and rejection of more modern and efficient wine-producing practices.

The most notable characteristic of Rioja wines today is a legacy of the French winemakers who were driven south by the phylloxeria blight of the late nineteenth century that destroyed their livelihood in France. They introduced aging in wood, and the oak-like, robust flavor of Riojas comes from comparatively long times in the barrel (a practice, ironically enough, the French no longer follow), after which the wine is mellowed even more by aging in bottles.

Typical red Riojas are aged for a minimum of two years in oak—and some for as long as six to nine years—before being bottled. The best Riojas, the *reservas*, may be aged in oak barrels up to 10 years. This long aging, coupled with another Rioja practice—leaving the juice in contact with the skins for long periods—makes for wines high in tannin that ultimately achieve wonderful depth and roundness. This means three things. First, Riojas tend to be big, full wines whose power comes from tannin and long aging. Second, large amounts of tannin give Riojas the potential to age ten to twenty years, and often longer, before showing any signs of breaking down. Third, because both regulations and tradition command long aging, Riojas are ready when you buy them. Although, as the *bodegas* (wine firms) now know, this aging is an extraordinary financial burden that winemakers in few other countries are willing to bear.

While the powerful Riojas are a dependable lot, there is another area of Spain where sophisticated—many say *the best*—winemaking takes place. This is the Penedès, a little to the south and west of Barcelona where the soil is rich with limestone and where Spain's famous sparkling wines are made. There are two great bodegas here: Torres, a family-owned company dating back to the seventeenth century; and Jean Leon, a newer and much smaller firm.

Most of the wine drunk in Spain is red, and while long aging works well with red wine, the Spanish have also traditionally applied the practice to whites. Old-style

Rioja whites may be aged from three to four years in oak, often resulting in heavy, woody, one-dimensional wines almost without fruitiness. At its worst, it tastes oxidized or like water stored for years in a cedar chest. In all fairness, the best old-style whites can also be substantial, full-flavored wines that many Europeans seem to prefer over the younger, thinner, crisper whites often prized by Americans. In recent years, more and more bodegas are producing both an old-style (aged) white and a new-style white that may have no wood aging at all. Unfortunately, you cannot tell which style you have just by looking at the label or the bottle. If the bottle is clear (rather than green), however, the color of the wine can be a giveaway. A deep yellow color invariably signals an old-style, aged white wine.

In the Rioja, two styles of red wine predominate: the *tinto*, a full-bodied, Burgundy-style red (often aged the longest); and the *clarete*, a lighter, more delicate, and sometimes fruitier wine. Both styles, because of the large amounts of tannin, accompany food very well and often need it to bring out the best in the wine. In fact, almost everyone in Spain seems to be nibbling something—such as those famous tiny hors d'oeuvres called *tapas*—when they drink red wine. (Tannin is softened by protein as, for example, when milk is put into tea, which also contains tannin.)

PORTUGAL

Eighty percent of all Portugal's wine exports are Mateus and Lancers, the two largest-selling brand name wines in the world. Another fifteen percent of Portugal's exports are other simple, easy drinking rosés. The remaining five percent is shared by Port, Muscatel, and some distinguished white and red wines, a few of which are exported.

Outside Portugal, there are two wines to be aware of: the *vinhos verdes* (literally, "green wines", actually meaning young wines) and the red wines from the Dão region. Vinhos verdes are readily available in liquor stores and in restaurants—and they are wonderful, slightly spritzy, low-alcohol wines, meant to be drunk young and rarely holding up more than two years.

The Dão River region is a rocky, difficult area with granitic soil, so the vines grown there must be exceptionally hardy. The resulting red wines are full-bodied and rich, with a deep, almost purple color. As in Spain, a certain amount of aging is standard—usually three years in cask and more in bottle. Good Dão wines are guaranteed by the Federation of Dão Viniculturists for place of origin.

Lastly, although Portugal's rosés are often looked down upon as unsophisticated, there are a few finds from small firms although they are rarely exported. These wines are clean, pleasant, and meant for easy drinking.

READING THE LABEL

Formerly, producers in the Rioja region believed that the stable climate created by protective mountain ranges plus careful blending between years combined to make vintage dating unimportant. In Spain, wine is still often sold without vintages and outside the regulations governing grape varieties. Wine exported to the United States, however, must meet strict regulations patterned after the French *Appellation d'Origine Contrôlée*. Now all Riojas exported to the United States are vintage-dated and carry the small, square Rioja seal that guarantees quality and proof of origin. Similarly, the wines of the Penedès are marked with a round *Denominación de Penedès* seal. Many other elaborate seals, referring to medals won in the last century, often appear on the labels. But the seal of *Denominación de Origen* is the reliable guarantee that the wine meets the government's strict regulations.

By and large, Spanish wines have always been blended, and thus—as is the case in Champagne—each house or, in this case, bodega, has a style or styles of its own. A bodega acquires its grapes from several winegrowers and sometimes will also have vineyards of its own, sometimes not. Aside from the Denominación de Origen seal, it

is the name of the bodega itself that assures you of the quality of the wine. Although experimenting with an unknown label can be worthwhile, a familiarity with the best bodegas is the most reliable way to select good Spanish or Portuguese wines.

The most exciting—and best value—Spanish wines are the reservas. The words Reserva, Gran Reserva, or Reserva Especial on a bottle of Rioja mean that the wine was made only from an exceptional harvest (1964 and 1970 are two of the best on the market today). Reservas are generally aged six to nine years in oak; and gran reservas and reservas especial, a minimum of nine and ten years respectively. Of course, Spaniards being the independent people that they are, each bodega usually has its own idea of the correct method for aging wine.

It should be noted that the term *Reserva* on a bottle of wine from the Penedès region does not mean the same thing as it does on a bottle of Rioja. In general, Penedès wines are aged much less; reserva here usually means grapes of superior quality.

GLOSSARY OF TERMS*

adega (P)–cellar or winery.

año (S)–age of wine when bottled; thus año 4° means that the wine was four years old when bottled.

blanco (S)–white.

bodega (S)–a winery, wine cellar, warehouse, or, more commonly, a wine shop.

branco (P)–white.

cepa (S)–wine or grape variety.

clarete (S)–light red wine.

colheita (P)–vintage.

cosecha (S)–vintage.

criado y embotellado por . . . (S)–grown and bottled by . . . .

doce (P)–sweet.

dulce (S)–sweet.

embotellado de origin (S)–estate bottled.

garrafeira (P)–matured in the bottle, usually an indication of quality.

maderized–wine that has been aged for a long time in the barrel. Sometimes a term of criticism.

madura (P)–mature, as opposed to young wine, or vinho verde.

medio-seco (S)–semidry.

rancio (S)–maderized white wine.

reserva (S)–wines that have been aged; usually an indication of quality.

rosado (S, P)–rosé.

seco (S, P)–dry.

tinto (S, P)–red.

vendimia (S)–vintage.

vinho verde (P)–literally "green wine" but means young wine.

*(P)–Portugal;   (S)–Spain

Bodegas Bilbainas Brillante Blanco Especial
80

This semidry grapey wine is sometimes too sweet for those who like crisp whites, but for parties, or even for making Sangria, it is an enjoyable, unsophisticated wine.

Bodegas Olarra Blanco Seco
79

A nice balance between the old and new styles of white Riojas, it has one year in oak but keeps its clean fresh taste with a touch of fruit. It is hard to believe that no sauvignon blanc grapes are in here, but the grapes are the native viura and malvasia.

Bodegas Olarra Cerro Añon
75

Only a year in wood, this wine has power and a full tannin taste. Dark garnet color, it has a lingering finish.

Bodegas Olarra Reciente
80

Light and lively, almost like a Fumé Blanc in character, this white wine has no wood aging, but it is well made and crisp. Easy drinking.

Bodegas Olarra Tinto
78, 76

Olarra is considered one of the most modern wineries in the world and is a perfectionist about winemaking. This very easy drinking red wine has a good fruity bouquet, is very open and fresh, and not typically woody. Light claret style.

Carvalho, Ribeiro, and Ferreira Conde de Santar Dáo
74

Enhanced by an open bouquet with good fruit and a little tannin, this red has nice body, reminiscent of the ordinary reds of Bordeaux. It is quite easy to drink; serve with meat dishes.

★ **Carvalho,** A fruity, full vinho verde, al-
Ribeiro, most like a French Muscadet,
and Ferreira but more spritzy and tart, this
Ravel wine would stand up well to
Vinho Verde most food and still maintain its
80 own character.

Compañia This very pleasant red is round,
Vinicola slightly fruity, not silky but
Del Norte full and well-balanced. Its
De España flavors linger. The year 1976
Rioja was considered excellent in the
78, 76 Rioja.

Compañia A good example of a traditional
Vinicola white Rioja, C.V.N.E. still ages
Del Norte its wines in wood, and this one
De España has that very dry, bold flavor
Rioja Blanco that comes from the white viura
80 grape. It is not fruity, but
strong enough to accompany
any sort of food.

Federico This white wine has excellent
Paternina acid / fruit balance. It has a
Banda Dorado crisp, refreshing quality, but is
82 not thin. Its very pleasing flow-
ery character has a hint of
vanilla. Serve with seafood, a
light lunch, or even bread and
cheese.

Gran Condal The deep golden color is char-
Rioja Blanco acteristic of wood-aged white
78 Riojas. It does not taste maderized but is definitely heavy
with some charm and fruit still
present.

López Steely dry and full-bodied, this
de Heredia traditional white Rioja has very
Viña Tondonia little fruit in its flavor. None-
Rioja Blanco theless, it has a solid, woody
75 character and long lasting
flavor.

★ **López de Heredia Viña Tondonia Rioja Tinto**
_76_, _75_

This very open red is almost as assertive as a Rhône, not meaty, but very well-balanced, and full in the mouth. It could accompany anything from chicken to roasts.

Marqués de Cáceres Blanco
_82_

An excellent, refreshing white, typical of the new style, without barrel aging, this is fresh and fruity, with a hint of almonds. It has good acidity and is pleasant enough by itself or with seafood.

Marqués de Riscal Blanco
_81_

A clean, well-made white with a certain chalky flavor, this Riscal is made—not in Rioja—but in Rueda, about 100 miles west, from native rueda grapes. It has a medium-heavy body, but no woodiness, and has a good dry bite and a long finish.

★ **Pedro Domecq Privilegio del Rey Sancho, Red**
_78_, _76_

Both 1978 and 1976 were excellent years in Rioja and you can find Privilegios from both vintages on the market. The 1978 is full, fruity, and promises even more with longer aging. Privilegio is aged in oak and in the bottle but not as long as has been traditional in the Rioja. Although this wine is soft and round, it is not woody.

Pedro Domecq Privilegio del Rey Sancho, White
_81_, _80_

The Domecqs, always famous in Spain for Sherry, began buying land in the prime Rioja Alavesa region in 1972. Unusual for Rioja bodegas, they use grapes only from their own vineyards. This white is fresh, crisp and full, and has no wood aging at all.

Quinta da Aveleda Vinho Verde An excellent example of a Portuguese vinho verde, this white is tart, crisp, and bone-dry with a lively spritzy character.

Torres Coronas 79 Torres is slowly making a reputation for itself as the finest bodega in Spain. This wine is their basic red—a combination of two local grapes. It has a soft, fresh flavor, good fruitiness, and just enough aging (1 year in oak, 1 in the bottle) to give it roundness and balance.

★ **Torres Viña Esmerelda** 81 Torres is well-known for its flair and experimentation, and this white is the best example. A combination of Alsacean muscat and gewürztraminer grapes, it has a big fruity aroma and is clean, full, and very refreshing.

WINES $5–10

★ **Bodegas Olarra Cerro Añon Gran Reserva** 70 A strong, big, fruity red, with a good chalky viscosity in the mouth and a long finish, this wine comes specifically from the Alavesa region in Rioja—known for full, round, Burgundy-style wines.

Bodegas Olarra Gran Reserva 70 The gran reserva has a bit more woody spice to it than the reserva. It also has a spendid finish and is an excellent red wine for meat or pasta. It is held by the bodega 11 years before release.

Bodegas Olarra Reserva
_73_

The Olarra reservas have consistently won international awards, and this red wine shows why. Aged 2 years in oak, 2 in the bottle, it is big but not heavy-handed. A perfect combination of light wood, chalkiness, and fruit, it is very clean and well balanced.

Carvalho, Ribeiro, and Ferreira Vinho Tinto Garrafeira
_70_

A remarkable Portuguese red wine with a touch of orange, this one is well balanced, mildly spicy, with a long finish and a notable crispness for a red wine. Garrafeira is a term that often signifies the producer's best.

Compañia Vinicola Del Norte De España Imperial Gran Reserva
_70_

A complex, interesting red, not completely balanced, but with an excellent, strong, woody character. Nonetheless, this has a tight, alcohol bouquet and a spicy chalk flavor which makes it zesty rather than silky. It may improve with more age.

Compañia Vinicola Del Norte De España Monopole
_79_

Monopole is one of the best-liked whites in Spain. It is easy to drink and amenable to any food because of its freshness and light body. Not as flat and dry as a traditional white Rioja, it is reminiscent of a well made Soave.

J. M. de Fonseca Periquita
_73_, _71_, _70_

The Portuguese firm of Fonseca is famous for Lancers, the second largest selling brand name in wine in the world. This wine, however, is Fonseca's serious wine: a deep ruby red, with a rich fruitiness to it and a little peppery spice.

Jean Leon Cabernet Sauvignon
77, 75, 73

This 100 percent Cabernet has a medium body with good blackcurrant fruitiness, some tannin, and a bit of astringency. In another 5 years it will be a great wine to serve with game or steak. Because it has been aged for 2 years in limousin oak, it has a nice softness.

Jean Leon Chardonnay
80, 79

Like Torres, Jean Leon plants chardonnay grapes in the Penedès region of Spain. This white is smooth and full-flavored—almost like a California Chardonnay but with a nuttiness that resembles Bordeaux. It is barrel-fermented in French limousin oak.

López de Heredia Viña Tondonia Reserva
70

A well-bred, firm, red wine that has a lively "attack" when you first sip it. Dark garnet color and more wood and chalkiness than fruit in the flavor, it is still a graceful wine at its peak and sure to give a lot of pleasure.

★ Marqués de Cáceres
78, 76

Cáceres, a bodega founded in 1970, makes lively, modern Riojas. This is one of their best: good, full, fruity, with the body of a Beaujolais.

Marqués de Cáceres Reserva
70

In 1970 many bodegas made reservas because of the quality of the vintage. This wine was aged 7 years in oak, then 2 years in the bottle, to produce a luscious, well-rounded, very smooth red, still with a touch of fruit.

Marqués de Riscal Blanco, Reserva Limousin _81_ When the traditional bodega Marqués de Riscal decided to make white wine, it built a new winery about 100 miles away from Rioja in a region called Rueda. This white, from Rueda's native verdejo grape, is crisp, but has a rounded chalky flavor that comes from 6 months of aging in limousin oak. It is quite delicious.

Marqués de Riscal Tinto _78_ Riscal, founded in 1860, is one of the most traditional Rioja firms, putting much emphasis on barrel aging. They also decant all of their wines from barrel to barrel 4 times a year rather than use modern filtration methods. The 1978 red is a light ruby color, with a slightly harsh bite. Though it seems to have a big structure, the taste is a little thin. Aged 3½ years.

Pedro Domecq Privilegio Reserva _76_ One of the best-value reservas, this red has a clean fruity style that is not diminished by 3 years in oak and 2 more in the bottle. The result is a medium-bodied, claret-style wine that is full and easy to like.

Torres Gran Coronas Reserva _77_ A cousin of the 1970 Black Label Gran Coronas which beat even Château Latour in the 1979 French Gault and Millau Wine Olympics, this is an exceptional red in its own right. With silky, dry berry flavor, it is nicely woody, but not overpowering, and has a superb, mellow, long finish.

Torres
Gran Sangre
de Toro Reserva
_77_

Torres' Sangre de Torre wines are robust, earthy and peppery—almost like Rhône wines in fullness and fruit. Deep, powerful, and high in alcohol, the regular, less expensive Sangre de Toro is aged in oak for a year. The Gran Sangre de Toro is aged for 2 years, comes from selected batches of grapes, and has enough tannin to ensure a long, luscious life.

Torres
Viña Santa Digña
_78_

This wine has one of the most powerful punches around—and not surprisingly, because Torres makes it from the famous Burgundy grape, pinot noir. Everything about this wine—color, aroma, flavor, finish—is intense. Serve with a hearty dish or a rich cheese.

Torres
Viña Sol
and
Gran Viña Sol
_82_, _81_

Both these white wines are a blend of the French chardonnay grape with a native Penedès white grape, the parellada. Clean, fruity, with a nice acidity, the 1982 has a bit more vanilla. A less expensive wine, Torres Viña Sol, is crisp, light, and easy-drinking. The regular Viña Sol and the more elegant Gran Viña Sol are both excellent wines for fish, fruit and cheese.

The United States

CALIFORNIA

*T*he honorable history of winemaking in California started with the planting of vines in the Missions in the mid-eighteenth century. The industry flourished until Prohibition imposed its fourteen-year hiatus upon winemaking. The resulting loss of vineyards and skilled winemakers meant that winemaking had to start again with repeal in 1933. The fresh start has made California wineries the most modern in the world, with the most advanced equipment and a modern approach to winemaking that does not suffer from the deadweight of tradition.

The way in which the wines of California are named also represents a split between the old and the new. The wines regarded as the finest, and which sell for the highest prices, are named after the main grape variety used (legally 75 percent or more since 1 January 1983). Examples are wines made from the chardonnay, barbera, and cabernet sauvignon grapes. The least expensive California wines (and the overwhelming majority in terms of volume produced) borrow their identities from their European heritage—Chablis, Burgundy, Sauterne—albeit often in a confusing and inaccurate way. Thus a wine from California labelled Sauterne (without the final "s") is *not* the equivalent of a Sauternes from the Bordeaux region of France. Instead of being a luscious, rich, sweet wine like a Sauternes, the California version is a white wine which probably, but not necessarily, is off-dry. Furthermore, it will be made from any grapes the vintner has on hand or chooses to use for that particular bottling. The same can be said for California Chablis which has no chardonnay in it and certainly is not like its French namesake. Nor does a California Burgundy have pinot noir or a Chianti any sangiovese.

In practice, the wines with these names from Europe (called *generic* as opposed to *varietal*) are usually not vintaged; that is, there is no date on the label and they are not necessarily from a single year's grapes. Most of these generics are blended with considerable skill not only so that they taste good but so that the Burgundy you buy this year will taste almost identical to the Burgundy of last year or three or four years ago.

If you want to know exactly what you are buying, want to find the same tastes as the bottle you have learned to like, then the nonvintaged wines of Gallo, Christian

Brothers, Masson, Almaden, and so on, are the ones for you. They are not poor wines, just good, sound, inexpensive wines for drinking now. They are everyday wines to have with dinner, to quaff or to sip as you will for sensual rather than intellectual pleasure.

Because of variations in soil, climate, and cultivation (pruning, spacing of vines, and so on), grapes differ according to where and how they are grown. Thus, there are regional differences between a cabernet grape grown in Napa or the Livermore Valley, a cabernet grown in Santa Barbara and one grown in the Pauillac and St.-Emilion regions in Bordeaux. The way the winemaker processes the grapes also affects the character of the wine: the length of contact the juice has with the skins, the type of fermentation, the strain of yeast used, the temperature of fermentation, the kinds and degree of clarification, the kinds of oak used during aging and the length of aging: an almost infinite number of factors can influence the final flavor and aroma.

It is almost impossible to identify the origin of the grapes by tasting California wines. There are just far too many variables for a regional identification of wines in the same manner as in much of Europe. The style of the winery is much more important than the region in shaping the wine, and it is the wineries rather than the regions that you should become familiar with to develop an appreciation of California wines.

Selecting only eighty or so wines means that many, many good ones were left out, sometimes simply because they are not widely available. Use this list as a starting point and experiment with offerings from lesser known wineries. They will probably be a wonderful adventure. (Some of these hard-to-find, good wines are listed without comment.)

Very few California wines merit the price stratosphere of $15 or more. (This does not refer to rarities.) The few wines that do fit into this price category are almost always in limited supply and difficult to get. Mainly they are Cabernet Sauvignon with a few Chardonnay and Pinot Noir wines. Justifiably in this price category because of the high cost of production are some of the late-harvested white (Johannisberg) Riesling wines that are the equivalent of Germany's Beerenauslese or Trockenbeerenauslese.

Almaden Vineyards Mountain Red Claret This red wine tastes much better than its fanciful name suggests. It is like a Pinot Noir, with soft, spicy flavor, and is a nice wine for the money.

Almaden Vineyards Sauvignon Blanc _81_ A magnificent bouquet first entrances you with this white. In the mouth, the flavors are balanced without anything done to extreme. Serve chilled.

Bel Arbes White Zinfandel An offering from Fetzer's second label, this white has the color of so many blanc de noirs, a light salmon. Pleasant, fruity flavors yet with some substance.

★ R & J Cook Varietal Red There are some first class varieties in this "generic" red wine. The result is an herbal fruitiness, good flavors, and some depth.

E & J Gallo Hearty Burgundy A mature, dry red wine of good depth, this has lots of fruitiness and soft texture.

★ E & J Gallo Sauvignon Blanc This white ranked very high in a recent panel tasting. It has clean flavors with good varietal character and engaging fruitiness.

Konocti Winery White Zinfandel _81_ The juice is separated from the dark skins of the zinfandel grape immediately to keep the color of this blanc de noirs light. The flavors are clean with a sweetness that is balanced with a good acid level. Drink as you would a fine rosé.

Le Bay Cellars Russian River Red _79_ Named after the area in the Sonoma Valley it comes from, this is a pleasant red wine, simple and easy to drink.

Le Fleuron Vin Blanc A second label from the very prestigious Joseph Phelps winery, this white has good, fruity aroma, medium body, a dry and lingering finish.

✴ **Louis M. Martini Pinot Noir** This red may not be a great Pinot Noir in the Burgundian tradition, but it is soft and bright, with a fruity flavor.

Robert Mondavi Winery White Table Wine
82
The slightly grassy aroma of this generic white suggests some sauvignon blanc in the blend. In the mouth it is round, of medium body, and has a dry finish.

★ **The Monterey Vineyard Classic California Red** In this red, there are well-balanced fruity flavors with surprising complexity for such an inexpensive wine. Youthful still, the wine is pleasing to drink now and has some future.

★ **Parducci Wine Cellars Chenin Blanc**
81
A clean and fruity white but one not stripped of its varietal character, it reflects a good application of modern technology.

Parducci Wine Cellars French Colombard
81
Fruity, soft flavors are made bright by a good acid level in this simple and most pleasant white wine.

Parducci Wine Cellars Mendocino County Chablis
81
There are fresh and fruity aromas to this white, with a lively, clean flavor and a slightly sweet finish.

San Pasqual Vineyards San Pasqual Red Here is an example of the latest trend of giving generic wines honest names like this instead of "copy cat" names, such as Burgundy. It is an easy-drinking red wine, round in the mouth.

Taylor California Classic Cabernet Sauvignon This red wine has a rich fruity bouquet and soft flavors that are distinctly cabernet in character. Drink now.

★ **Trefethen Vineyards Eshcol Red** This medium-bodied wine has a rich, fruity aroma, evident when the wine is poured into the glass. Its soft feel in the mouth shows it is mature and ready to drink even though it may improve a little in the bottle.

WINES $5–10

Concannon Vineyard Muscat Blanc 79 Lively flavors of the muscat grape, that are just off-dry (meaning a touch of sweetness), combine in this white to create a fruity and well-balanced wine.

Estrella River Winery Muscat Canelli 81 There are traces of peaches and oranges in the bouquet of this white. In flavor it is slightly sweet but with a wonderful balance so that it is not cloying.

Fetzer Vineyards Mendocino Cabernet Sauvignon 80 A balanced, soft-flavored Cabernet, this red will drink better next year and for several after that.

★ **Guenoc Ranch Cabernet Sauvignon** <u>80</u> Here is a soft, fruity-flavored cabernet, but the finish dries out the mouth. This red wine is drinkable now but will improve for several years.

★ **Gundlach-Bundschu Winery Merlot** <u>80</u> In this red there is the typical full fruitiness of merlot and enough substance underneath to make it attractive. It is nice now but will get better in the next 2 to 3 years, perhaps as many as 5.

Hacienda Wine Cellars Gewürztraminer <u>81</u> There is a spicy, tart flavor in this dry white wine which finishes with a bitter edge that is quite pleasant.

Kenwood Vineyards Pinot Noir Blanc <u>82</u> A soft, pleasant blanc de noirs with a good finish, it should be drunk now or within a year.

Kenwood Vineyards Sauvignon Blanc <u>81</u> Here is a typical example of sauvignon blanc: a dry wine, soft on the palate, round in the mouth; excellent balance.

Mirassou Vineyards White Burgundy <u>82</u> This white is not from Burgundy, of course, but rather from Mendocino. It has a nice floral bouquet, round flavors, and just a hint of sweetness.

Robert Mondavi Winery Chenin Blanc <u>81</u> A good and typical example of Chenin Blanc, this one possesses engaging aromas, good clean flavors, and a slightly sweet finish.

Robert Mondavi Winery Johannisberg Riesling 82
Somewhat reminiscent of a Rheingau, this Riesling has an apple-like bouquet, and well-balanced, spicy flavors.

★ **The Monterey Vineyard Johannisberg Riesling** 82
The bouquet of this Riesling is perfumey and reminiscent of muscat. This white wine has a lively fruit flavor with a slight sweetness.

★ **J. Pedroncelli Vineyards Gewürz-traminer** 81
The strong flavors of this gewürztraminer are loaded with fruit—a wine with a slightly sweet finish.

★ **Simi Winery Chardonnay** 80
A wine whose richness indicates it has substance but does not overwhelm you, this white has long warm finish after you swallow.

Vose Vineyards Zinblanca (White Zinfandel) 82
Billed by the winemaker as "the world's greatest popcorn wine," this white is good even without popcorn.

H A R D   T O   F I N D

Ballard Canyon Winery Cabernet Sauvignon Blanc (W) 82

Ballard Canyon Winery Johannisberg Riesling (W) 81

Boeger Winery Merlot (R) 80

Buehler Vineyard Zinfandel (R) 80

Chateau St. Jean Johannisberg Riesling (W) 81

Clos Du Bois Johannisberg Riesling (W) 81

Edmeades Vineyard Gewürztraminer (W) 81

Felton-Empire Gewürztraimer (W) 81

Glen Ellen Winery Cabernet Sauvignon (R) 81

Grand Cru Vineyard Dry Chenin Blanc (W) 81

Keenan Winery Merlot (R) 78

Leeward Winery Coral (Pinot Noir Blanc) (W) 82

Los Vineros Chenin Blanc (W) 81

Lower Lake Winery Cabernet Sauvignon (R) 79

Madroña Vineyards Cabernet Sauvignon (R) 79

Parsons Creek Chardonnay (W) 81

Pine Ridge Cabernet Sauvignon (R) 80

Raymond Vineyards Zinfandel (R) 79

Ridge Vineyards Zinfandel (R) 79

Santa Barbara Winery White Zinfandel (W) 82

Ventana Vineyard Chenin Blanc (W) 81

Zaca Mesa Winery Sauvignon Blanc (W) 81

(R) red; (W) white

WINES $10–15

Acacia Winery Chardonnay A winery that has shot into prominence in a very short time has produced a Chardonnay white of great depth, wonderful balance, and a lingering finish.

Chateau Montelena Cabernet Sauvignon
_79_

There are rich and fruity flavors in this red wine but it has a bite that will soften with more bottle age. Good now, it will be better later.

★ **Chateau St. Jean Fumé Blanc**
_82_

An elegant white, typical of the variety, it is fresh, fruity and rich without excess.

Clos Du Val Merlot
_79_

This winery took rich, ripe fruit to make this red wine and the richness shows—there is great depth. Drink now, but will improve with keeping.

★ **Concannon Vineyard Cabernet Sauvignon**
_77_

Not many Cabernets come from the Livermore Valley. This red wine has no special attributes, it is just a fine cabernet.

Jekel Vineyard Cabernet Sauvignon
_79_

A drinkable red, this will be much better with a year or more aging. It has soft, fruity, well-balanced flavors with some tannins showing that promise a good future.

Robert Keenan Winery Merlot
_79_

There are lovely hints of raspberries and mint in the bouquet of this flavorful, balanced red. It has the potential for 5 or more years aging.

Kenwood Vineyard Chardonnay Beltane Ranch
_80_

The chardonnay grapes from Beltane Ranch in the Sonoma Valley show up well vintage after vintage, producing clean, rich flavors in this specially labelled Kenwood Chardonnay.

★ **Kenwood Vineyards Chardonnay** 81 — Not quite as full-flavored or oaky as the Beltane Ranch version, this white has good varietal character.

Rutherford Hill Winery Chardonnay 80 — A winery noted for its fruity wines has produced this white which is silky in texture and has buttery flavors.

★ **Sequoia Grove Vineyards Chardonnay** 80 — From one of the younger, smaller wineries, this white wine is a little tart, complex, and almost oily on the palate in its butteriness.

Z-D Wines Cabernet Sauvignon 80 — This small winery moved from Sonoma to Napa but the quality of its wines keeps improving. Rich flavor in this Cabernet says it all.

Z-D Wines Chardonnay 81 — Just drinkable now, this Chardonnay has plenty of room for improvement with a year or so more bottle age. This white has rich, clean flavors and a creamy texture.

H A R D   T O   F I N D

Ballard Canyon Cabernet Sauvignon (R) 80

Chateau St. Jean Chardonnay (W) 80

Chateau St. Jean Fumé Blanc (W) La Petite Etoile 82

Davis Bynum Winery Chardonnay (W) Allen-Hafner Reserve 81

Durney Vineyard Cabernet Sauvignon (R)

Fetzer Vineyards Chardonnay (W) Special Reserve 81

Preston Vineyards Sauvignon Blanc (W) 80

Acacia Winery A bright cherry red of medium
Pinot Noir depth and a fruity bouquet, its
Lee Vineyard flavors are soft and fruity.
<u>81</u>

Beringer A red wine with a rich, bright,
Vineyards and clear color, this one has a
Cabernet heady bouquet of fruit and
Sauvignon alcohol. The tastes are soft with
Private Reserve lots of rich fruit with good
<u>78</u> balance; excellent finish.

David Bruce Green-gold in color with an
Winery expansive, fruity, varietal bou-
Chardonnay, quet and a hint of tobacco, this
estate bottled white has subtle tastes, with a
<u>81</u> blending of Chardonnay flav-
ors and excellent oak aging. It
is soft on the palate, quite
pleasant.

Buena Vista Though 4 years old, this
Winery cabernet still shows a purple
Cabernet edge to its medium-dark red
Sauvignon color, which is a sign of its rela-
Special Selection tive youth. The bouquet is still
<u>79</u> undeveloped but shows much
promise. Pronounced varietal
fruitiness, it drinks fairly easily now but should be kept 3 to
5 years before opening.

Burgess Cellars A red wine with a rich, bright
Cabernet bouquet and a soft, well-
Sauvignon, balanced, fruity flavor that is
Vintage Select characteristic of the best Cali-
<u>79</u> fornia Cabernets.

Chalone The bouquet of this white
Vineyard speaks of oak and chardonnay
Chardonnay married well. There are ex-
<u>81</u> cellent intense flavors in fine
balance but it is the lingering
and complex finish that really
gives this wine class.

Clos du Bois Chardonnay 81 — A light green-gold color and a rich and complex set of aromas are most appealing about this white wine. The soft, fruity chardonnay flavors are notable for their finesse and balance.

Kenwood Vineyard Cabernet Sauvignon, Artist Series 79 — The winemaker claims long life for this red wine, "approaching 20 years." Because of its balance it should last this long, but it will be supple enough to drink by the end of this decade.

Monterey Peninsula Cabernet Sauvignon 79 — Medium-bright color with a good cabernet bouquet distinguish this red. It has bright, fruity, varietal flavors.

Raymond Vineyards Cabernet Sauvignon 79 — A red wine with such rich fruitiness that it seems sweet even though bone dry, it is good for drinking now but will last for 5 or more years.

★ **Z-D Wines Cabernet Sauvignon** 79 — The intensity of this Cabernet is tempered by almost 25 percent merlot grapes, giving it a rich fruitiness. A dark-colored red wine, bright in aspect, its bouquet is still developing. It combines elegance and intensity and has at least a 10-year future.

EASTERN UNITED STATES

East of the Rocky Mountains, there are almost four hundred wineries scattered from Texas to New England, Minnesota to the Deep South. This rather large area happens to be home to a third of all the species of grapevines known around the world. Naturally, it grows the most diverse group of wines of any wine district on earth. Old American varieties such as catawba, delaware and concord come to mind first, with their urgent, grapey flavors. Down South the traditional wine comes from native muscadine grapes like the scuppernong.

But the most exciting wines are in the East and belong to a new generation of vineyards planted since World War II. They grow the vinifera varieties of Europe (and California) and hybrids from European-American crosses. Led by New York State's Finger Lakes, the Northeast in particular is establishing a reputation for crisp, fruity white wines. The East's relatively cool climate retains the natural acidity in grapes, producing tart wines often balanced by vintners with a touch of residual sweetness. They are generally lighter-bodied and livelier than California wines—closer to the German style or the wines of France's Loire Valley, with some notable Burgundian exceptions.

Most of the best wines from east of the Rockies are white. The varietals Seyval

Blanc, Chardonnay, Vidal Blanc, and Sauvignon Blanc, usually vinified dry, stand out as some of America's finest seafood wines. Eastern Riesling, Cayuga White, Delaware, and Ravat are generally softer, emphasizing the flavors of sweet ripe fruit.

Vintages have been remarkably consistent in recent years with 1980 and 1982 considered outstanding in many districts, 1978 and 1981 are generally very good. Longevity is rarely an asset. Almost all these wines, including the reds, are best in their youth: one to three years old for the whites and rosés, two to five for the reds.

The big problem with eastern American wines is availability. Some of their wines can only be purchased directly from the winery (although often United Parcel Service and mailorder delivery can be arranged). But as the new, quality estates grow, and the big, established producers turn more of their attention to grape varieties that make world-class wines, consumers should find it easier to spot at least some of these wines on the local retail shelf.

WINES UNDER $5

Cascade Mountain Vineyards Reserved Red
New York
81, 80

Dark purple color and the suggestion of wild grasses in the smell and taste are typical of red, French-American hybrids. Some complexity has been achieved here by blending, and this is a well-balanced wine,

with clean, ripe fruit flavors, and nice finish.

Fenn Valley Vineyards Vidal Blanc
Michigan
82, 81

Michigan has made a specialty of this hybrid variety, and this farm winery is the pacesetter. The white has a fresh, citric aroma, and some sweetness balanced with a crisp edge. The reserve version is meatier.

★ Gold Seal Vineyards Dry Riesling
New York
81

Light and delicate, this white wine is still a full representation of varietal Riesling character. There are nuances of peaches and apples in the aroma. It is not entirely dry but is a good food wine and an exceptional bargain. The regular Johannisberg Riesling is sweeter, more expensive, but also good value.

Mt. Pleasant Seyval Blanc
Missouri
82

A clean, simple, bone-dry seafood white wine with grassy overtones, it comes from the first viticultural district officially declared by the U.S. government.

Poplar Ridge Vineyards Valois Blanc
New York
82, 81

A sensitive blend of French hybrid and American varieties puts a stylish, semidry frame around the perfume and luscious flavor of Delaware, the dominant variety in this white wine.

Sakonnet Vineyards Compass Rosé
Rhode Island

This lovely amber-colored rosé is fresh, clean, crisp, and fairly dry for rosé, and makes a good light luncheon wine. Sakonnet is also known for elegant Chardonnay and tart white blends matched well with local seafood.

Taylor Lake Country Chablis
New York

Taylor's newly released competition for Almaden and Gallo is this white. It is a blend of several French-American varieties, vinified dry, but with plenty of fruit and natural acidity.

WINES $5–10

Benmarl Vineyards Marlboro Village Red
New York

Medium-bodied blend of hybrid varieties in the style of *village* wines of Burgundy, for which it could be mistaken. This red wine has round, woody overtones, and typically (for hybrids) a short finish.

Byrd Vineyards Sauvignon Blanc
Maryland
81, 80, 79

In the Fumé style, there are plenty of woody flavors here that trim the characteristic grassy taste of this variety when picked very ripe. It is a tart and astringent white, with a peppery aftertaste.

★ Glenora Seyval Blanc
New York
82, 81, 80

A ripe, floral aroma and crisp, dry, citric flavors with a suggestion of fresh peaches characterize this pale, rather austere, white wine. It comes from one of the eastern leaders also known for their Riesling and Chardonnay. Serve with seafood.

Hargrave Vineyards Sauvignon Blanc
New York
81, 80

A crisp, well-balanced white, it has an assertive, herbal varietal character without overripe weediness, and a fine, spicy finish. Fumé Blanc is the same wine transformed with barrel aging, with equal success.

Heron Hill Ravat
New York
82, 81, 80

This lesser-known but most promising French-American variety is capable of developing complexity in the bottle. This white has a typical grapefruit quality, lively acidity, and is well-balanced with semidry finish.

Konstantin Frank Vinifera Wine Cellars Gewürztraminer
New York
80, 78

Frank, the man who pioneered the successful cultivation of European grapes in the eastern U.S., 30 years ago, continues to make benchmark Riesling, Chardonnay and Gewürztraminer. The latter is a deeply colored, musky, spicy wine, fairly dry, with an elegant finish.

Llano Estacado Cabernet Sauvignon
Texas

This landmark red wine shows great promise in Texas for a classic vinifera table wine. It has a clean, herbal varietal character, a deep garnet color, and medium body, with the structure to continue improving.

★ **Meredyth Vineyards October Harvest**
Virginia
82, 81

Here is a fat, off-dry white wine with an abundance of fruit-salad flavors. It has sufficient acid to mate well with rich seafoods and shellfish. Varietal seyval blanc comes through.

Nashoba Valley Dry Blueberry
Massachusetts

This genuinely dry but fruity, medium-bodied dinner wine bears an astonishing resemblance to Zinfandel. It comes from an innovative producer who is committed to resurrecting the American heritage of fruit wines.

Otter Spring Johannisberg Riesling
New York
82, 81, 80

An expansive, floral aroma suggests German Mosel and carries through in delicate but complex varietal fruit flavors in this white wine. Moderate sweetness is supported with acidity. There are honey tones in some years from natural *bot tis* mold on the grapes.

Stone Hill Norton
Missouri
79

An old Missouri variety in renaissance in this red. It has a full-bodied fruit flavor, with peppery anise overtones, harmonizing in wood-aged maturity. With a clean, complex finish, it will continue to improve.

★ **Wickham Vineyards Cayuga White**
New York
82, 81

Pale straw color and a light, fresh aroma belie the intense, mouth-filling flavors of lemon and orange in this white wine.

Woodbury A white wine of genuine
Vineyards balance, this has an acidic
Seyval Blanc backbone, yet is soft, full of
New York fruit. Dry, with medium body,
81, 80 it is excellent with poultry.

WINES $10–15

Gold Seal This first commercial vinifera
Vineyards white wine from the eastern
Chardonnay U.S. is still one of the best.
New York Medium-yellow, it is aromatic
82, 81, 80 and loaded with chardonnay
fruit that is filled out with
supple oak overtones.

Markko The taste of this deep-gold-
Vineyards colored white wine reflects the
Chardonnay earnest use of old American oak
Lake Erie, which overwhelms varietal fruit,
Ohio bringing out buttery, lemony
80, 79 flavors. It has high alcohol and
extract, and a long, elegant
aftertaste tinged with almond
bitterness.

Wagner Here is a big, well-constructed
Vineyards wine, layered with fruit-and-nut
Chardonnay varietal flavors, with pro-
New York nounced but secondary tones
82, 81, 80 of French oak. Perfectly
balanced, it is dry but with a
surprising sweetness in the
aftertaste. Wagner also produces consistently fine Riesling
and Seyval Blanc.

Sparkling WINES

S parkling wines are best drunk young and fresh at festive occasions; they are better served as accompaniments to events than food. Although champagne is justifiably the most famous, there are many sparkling wines—mousseux, Schaumwein, spumante, sekt, espumoso.

The "sparkle" that gives these sparkling wines their lively, festive spirit is created by bubbles of carbon dioxide (CO_2) escaping from the wine. This effervescence is produced by one of two methods: carbonation or fermentation.

Carbonation is simply pumping carbon dioxide into the still wine under pressure, as is done with soda, and the quality of these sparkling wines tends to be on about the same level. Made by the cheapest method, using the cheapest base material, they are very poor substitutes for wines made to sparkle naturally through the fermentation process.

Normally, during fermentation, sugar in

the grape juice is converted into alcohol, and carbon dioxide is given off. In an open container, the gas escapes into the air; in a closed container, the resulting carbon dioxide is trapped in the wine, producing a natural "sparkle."

Besides carbon dioxide, fermentation deposits a sediment of solid particles, and this must be removed to produce a clean, clear, sparkling wine. In the *Charmat* (tank or bulk method) the fermentation takes place in a closed, pressurized vat, and this poses very little problem. The sediment is allowed to settle to the bottom of the tank, and the wine is clarified, drawn off its sediment, filtered, and bottled under pressure.

In the United States, wine made this way can be labelled "Champagne" (incorrectly), but the label must also indicate the method of production with such words as bulk fermented or Charmat process.

The better sparkling wines undergo two fermentations. The second takes place in the bottle, and in this case, the sediment is a bit harder to remove without also losing the effervescence. The easiest and least expensive method is by transferring the contents of the bottle, under pressure, to a large, pressurized vat where the sediment precipitates out; the wine is then clarified, filtered, and rebottled under pressure. This is the transfer method. The sparkling wine is fermented in bottle but cleared in tank. Wines made by this method often carry

"fermented in *the* bottle" (our emphasis) on the label, to distinguish them from tank-fermented wines and perhaps to link them with wines made by the champagne method which sometimes state, "fermented in *this* bottle" (our emphasis) on the label.

None of these methods produce true champagne. Champagne is made only by the champagne method, *méthode champenoise*. By this process, developed in Champagne, the northernmost wine region of France, the wine is given its second fermentation in the bottle and is cleared of its sediment by two steps: *remuage* and *dégorgement*. The bottles, held in riddling racks, are periodically shaken, twisted, and gradually turned *(remuage)* until they are nearly upside down so that all the sediment is collected in the neck of the bottle against the temporary cork, or crown cap.

In *dégorgement*, the next step, the cork is removed and the collected sediment allowed to shoot out under pressure, taking care to lose as little wine as possible.

Before final corking, the champagne is topped up with the same wine (for the driest style) or a *dosage* of wine and sugar. The amount of sugar in the *dosage* determines the degree of sweetness in the wine.

The preëminence of champagne among sparkling wines has led to some confusion and misuse of its name. In the United States and many other New World countries, such as Australia, the term *champagne* is frequently used simply to designate a wine with bubbles. Although all champagne is sparkling wine, all sparkling wine is definitely not champagne. True champagne is produced only in the Champagne region in France by the *méthode champenoise* process; in western Europe only these wines may carry the label "champagne".

BUYING SPARKLING WINES

There are not many good sparkling wines for under $10. Generally, the best in this price category are from France, although there are a few from Italy, California, and Spain. Most sparkling wines under $10 are made by either the cheaper, transfer or bulk method and are generally also produced from cheaper, inferior grapes.

No matter what the method, if the wine is sparkling, the U.S. taxation is considerable: $3.40 per gallon . Subtracting the cost of the bottle, cork, and packaging, there is not a lot left over for the producer to buy quality grapes and still keep the price under $10. All the wines we recommend in this chapter are fairly priced for their quality, which ranges from good to excellent; a few, those marked with a ★, are bargains.

Sparkling

FRANCE, CHAMPAGNE

Champagne is made in a variety of styles. The best are dry or brut. Champagne—true champagne—is fresh and balanced, rich and lively. No matter how full-bodied, champagne has a certain delicacy. These characteristics are rarely found in any other sparkling wines no matter what the description on the label says.

In champagne, the bubbles (or the bead) will be tiny, profuse, fast rising, and long lasting. The color will be pale straw to light gold, or shell pink to pale rosé, pure and limpid; the bouquet, enticing and complex.

A nonvintage brut will be fresh, with a restrained fruitiness and a yeasty character that recalls fresh bread. Brut vintage has a more complex bouquet; it will be richer and deeper, sometimes with a toasty quality, and with more complexity.

On the palate, champagne is clean, refreshing, even stimulating. The brut nonvintage is livelier and fresher than the vintage brut, which has a smooth, even creamy texture, and a more mellow nature from spending longer time on the yeast than nonvintage brut. The finish of the wine is clean and lingering. This overall character will vary, of course, from house to house.

The six main styles of champagne shipped to the United States are: brut nonvintage, brut vintage, extra dry, blanc de blancs,

rosé, and prestige cuvée. The last is the finest a firm has to offer.

Vintage brut champagnes are made only in years when the harvest is exceptional, and naturally they achieve a greater distinction than the nonvintage blends, where consistency from year to year is produced by skillful blending.

Extra dry champagnes are less dry and somewhat less refined than brut. As the name implies, blanc de blancs is made only from white grapes—the chardonnay. (Most champagne is a blend of black and white grapes.) In style, a blanc de blancs combines delicacy with finesse and elegance; and for some firms it is their prestige cuvée.

Rosé champagnes are generally fuller, more flavorful, and a little drier than a brut from the same house. Some houses vintage-date their rosé.

Rarely less than $40, and often $50 or more, a prestige cuvée is the best champagne produced by a firm. Generally, they are wines with most character, delicacy, and elegance—champagnes to contemplate or to serve on very special occasions. Since they are not drunk often, they do not have a high turnover rate; individual bottles are frequently sold when they are too old and have lost much of their finer qualities. With these wines it is more important than ever to select a bottle from a fresh shipment and a reliable shop.

Brut Nonvintage Champagne

Billecart-Salmon—light, delicate, and elegant.

Charles Heidsieck — medium-bodied, creamy, classic.

Moët et Chandon—light, fruity, fresh, lively.

Mumm—medium bodied, clean, fruity, toward a sweeter style than most bruts.

★ **Pol Roger**—classic, balanced, rich and smooth.

Pommery & Greno—light, dry, crisp, and firm.

Blanc de Blancs Champagne

★ **Robert Billion**—light and delicate, elegant and balanced; especially good value.

Extra Dry Champagne

Moët et Chandon—in the midrange for dryness/sweetness.

Mumm—a sweeter style.

Pommery & Greno—a drier style.

Brut Nonvintage Champagne

★ **Gosset**—classic, creamy, full, rich, and deep.

Brut Vintage Champagne

Vintages: <u>78</u>, <u>76</u>, <u>75</u>

Bollinger—full, rich, and creamy.

Moët et Chandon—light and fruity.

Pol Roger—classic, rich, and smooth.

Pommery & Greno—light, dry, and crisp.

Blanc de Blancs Champagne

Billecart-Salmon—very fine and very delicate, even fragile; the epitome of the type.

★ **Dom Ruinart**—refined, delicate, and subtle; a good buy.

★ **Jacquesson**—in the midrange for sweetness, lively; a very good buy.

Pol Roger Blanc de Chardonnay—a fuller though still delicate style.

Robert Billion, vintage-dated—delicate and elegant; especially fine value.

Salon, 1973—a full and rich style for a blanc de blancs, and an especially fine champagne.

Rosé Champagne
Vintages: <u>78</u>, <u>76</u>, <u>75</u>

Billecart-Salmon—delicate, elegant.

Gosset—smooth-textured and fruity, with some delicacy.

Moët et Chandon—a fruity style, with a hint of raspberries.

Philipponnat—a delicate floral bouquet, medium-bodied, firm.

Pol Roger—fruity, dry, with a smooth texture.

Prestige Cuvée Champagne
Recommended years: <u>76</u>, <u>75</u>, in some instances <u>73</u> or <u>71</u> (if you know the storage).

Bollinger Tradition R.D. (<u>73</u> is good)—dry, firm, rich, and creamy. Check the *dégorgement* date; up to 2 or 3 years after is safe.

Dom Pérignon—refined, elegant, balanced, and stylish.

Gosset Grand Millésime (<u>73</u> is still fine)—rich and intense, complex and creamy; for lovers of full, rich champagnes.

★ **Pol Roger Reserve Special** (<u>73</u> is still good)—creamy texture, stylish, and well-balanced.

Taittinger Comtes de Champagne—elegant, light, gentle.

California sparkling wines tend to be heavier, fruitier, softer, and sweeter in style than true champagnes. There is a trend, however, among producers of méthode champenoise wines toward a leaner, better balanced wine. Many of California's sparkling wines are now made by méthode champenoise (frequently employing machines for the riddling and degorging), although most are still made by the bulk process.

The *vins mousseux*, or sparkling wines from France, are made outside of Champagne, and are generally restrained in fruitiness, with a balance, lightness, and freshness. The majority of those not carrying an *Appellation d' Origine Contrôlée* (AC) are made by the bulk process; the AC sparkling wines use méthode champenoise and the best-known of these are from the Loire Valley.

Sekt, the most generally exported sparkling wine from Germany, is usually a light fresh wine with a noticeable sweetness. The majority are made by the Charmat method.

The *brut spumanti* or sparkling wines of Italy are generally light, balanced, and dry, occasionally austere and lean. The vast majority are made by the Charmat method, but there is a growing trend toward using the *metodo champenois*.

Spanish sparkling wines tend toward a fuller, rounder, and softer style, and are given longer aging on the yeast, than most of the sparkling wines from other countries. While often they do not appeal to our tastes, they are hard to beat for the price. The best are made by the champagne method (*cava*) and are from the following producers: Cordorniu, Conde de Caralt, Marques de Monistrol, and Paul Cheneau.

WINES UNDER $10

Asti Spumante
These bulk-fermented sparkling wines are from the Asti region. They have a fresh, fragrant, fruity aroma, often peach-like, sometimes reminiscent of pineapple or melon. Always light-bodied and fruity, reflecting the muscat grape, they are sweet, but the degree of sweetness varies. Best drunk as young as possible.
Producers: Cinzano (a sweeter style); Contratto (a drier style); Fontanafredda (in the midrange of sweetness); Martini & Rossi (medium sweet)

Baron Maurice Blanc de Blancs Brut
A medium-bodied sparkling wine with a slightly *goût de terroir* character, this is at the sweeter end of the brut range of vins mousseux.

★ Crémant de Bourgogne
Burgundy AC
At its best, this light vin mousseux has some delicacy, is fresh and balanced, and clean and dry, with a light yeastiness.
Producers: The two best buys are: Cramandor (Caves de Bailly), an especially fine value;

and Labouré Gontard (over $10 in some markets)

Crémant de Loire
Loire AC
A light-bodied, fruity vin mousseux this is clean and lively; the best have some delicacy.
Producer: Sablant

Duval Brut A reliable sparkling wine, it has a bread-like, yeasty aroma and is light in body and fruity, in the sweeter style for a brut vin mousseux.

★ Equipe 5 Brut, 1979 A metodo champenois spumante with a fruity, yeasty aroma, is light-bodied and smooth in texture. Its quality and price make it a best buy.

Korbel Brut This dryish, fruity wine is in the characteristic California style, but better balanced than most, not heavy.

Korbel Natural Similar to the brut but drier, this is a good choice for those who like the soft, round, fruity California style.

La Versa Pinot Oltrepò Pavese Spumante This Charmat spumante has a fruity aroma. It is light-bodied, clean, with noticeable sweetness balanced with sufficient acidity.

★ Saumur Mousseux
Loire AC
Similar to Vouvray Mousseux but generally fuller in body and softer, it is fruity and off-dry, balanced with good acidity.
Producers: Bouvet Brut (over $10 in some markets); Gratien

(has a slightly herbaceous background); Veuve Amiot Brut

Touraine Mousseux
Loire AC

Similar to but perhaps a little lighter than the other sparkling wines of the Loire this is light-bodied and agreeable, with a clean, fresh character, occasionally with a note of apples.
Producers: Brut de Mosny (over $10 in some markets); Monmousseau Brut

★ Vouvray Mousseux
Loire AC

Lighter and firmer than the sparkling wine of Saumur, this is generally off-dry or lightly sweet, with a somewhat fruity aroma, sometimes suggesting quince. The Vouvray region produces the best sparkling wines of the Loire.
Producers: Monmousseau (over $10 in some markets); Prince Poniatowski "Aigle d'Or"

WINES $10–20

Ca'del Bosco Franciacorta Pinot Brut Spumante

Light-bodied and moderately fruity, this dry spumante wine is made by the champagne method. It has a lightly yeasty aroma and a clean refreshing aftertaste.

Ca'del Bosco Franciacorta Pinot Dosage Zero Spumante

Similar to the Brut but drier and firmer, with some delicacy, this is made with the same grape varieties (pinot noir, pinot blanc, chardonnay) as the Brut.

Chandon Napa Valley Blanc de Noirs

Light shell pink (from 100 percent pinot noir grapes) with a fruity aroma, this California wine is dryish, agreeable and soft.

Chandon Napa Valley Brut Somewhat lighter in body than the Blanc de Noirs, the brut is drier but with a similar fruity nature and is soft and smooth.

Contratto Brut Spumante Light-bodied sparkling wine (metodo champenois), lean and firm with a nice crispness, sometimes even austere. It has a light yeasty character and a lingering finish.

Ferrari Brut de Brut Spumante Dry and firm all-chardonnay (blanc de blancs) spumante, with a smooth, almost creamy texture. (Like all Ferrari sparkling wines it is made metodo champenois.)

Fürst von Metternich Riesling Dry Sekt A lightly sweet and well-balanced wine (made by the champagne method), it has a perfumed floral aroma and is a good wine also beneath the bubbles.

Korbel Blanc de Blancs Korbel's top California wine has a fruity, floral aroma with a light yeasty character. It is light to medium in body, fruity, and balanced with good acidity.

Korbel Blanc de Noirs Not really a blanc de noirs (white wine from black grapes) this California sparkling wine is a rosé. It has a fruity aroma, with notes of yeast and vanilla, and is off-dry with some firmness.

Kupferberg Gold Deutscher Sekt Fairly full-bodied for a sekt, this dryish and balanced wine is made from good base material (by the transfer method).

Langenbach Waldracher Riesling Deutscher Sekt Ruwer Cuvée This wine has a fresh, fruity aroma and flavor, with noticeable riesling character. It is lightly sweet and well-balanced with lively acidity.

Mirassou Au Natural This undosed California sparkling wine is bone dry, firm and crisp, lean, even somewhat austere. The aroma has a lightly yeasty aspect.

Mirassou Blanc de Noirs This Blanc de Noirs is somewhat more yeasty in character than the Brut or Au Natural and though fruity, it is more restrained and is medium-bodied, well balanced, and lively.

Mirassou Brut Similar to the Au Natural but with more alcohol and body, this is also fruitier and rounder. It has a clean aroma with a slightly yeasty character.

Mirassou L.D.
(Late Disgorged) Essentially the same wine as the Brut, this one has two additional years on the yeast, which makes it a rounder, softer wine with more yeast character.

Sebastiani Sonoma Brut With a lightly yeasty aroma, this medium-bodied wine is clean and fresh, with an understated fruitiness for a California wine.

WINES OVER $20

Chandon Special Reserve Napa Valley Brut A refined, somewhat yeasty bouquet and a round, creamy texture characterize this well-balanced California sparkling wine. It also has a lingering finish. Available only in magnums.

Schramsberg Blanc de Noirs Made from white as well as black grapes, this is not a true blanc de noirs. It has a clean, fruity aroma, with a yeasty, breadlike aspect, and is medium-bodied, well-balanced, and fruity in an understated way for a California sparkling wine.

Schramsberg Reserve Napa Valley A wine with balance, style, and character, this is overall an impressive California sparkling wine. It has a somewhat fuller body and more forthright character than the Chandon Reserve.

INDEX

THE CONTRIBUTORS

France:

Harriet Lembeck is the director of the Wine/Beverage Program at the Waldorf-Astoria in New York City. A frequent contributor to *Les Amis du Vin*, *Beverage Media*, and other wine magazines, she recently completed the revision of Grossman's Guide to Wines, Beers, and Spirits.

Italy & Sparkling Wines:

Sheldon & Pauline Wasserman, regular contributors to *Vintage*, are the authors of five books on wine: The Wines of Italy, The Wines of the Côtes-du-Rhône, White Wines of the World, The Guide to Fortified Wines, and The Guide to Sparkling Wines.

Germany:

Terry Theise lived in Germany for several years when he travelled and studied German wines and wine-making. He lectures on German wine and is a contributor to *Decanter* and *Les Amis du Vin*.

Spain & Portugal:

Karen MacNeil writes on food, wine, and restaurants for *Food and Wine*, *Travel and Leisure*, *Gentlemen's Quarterly*, and *American Health*. She currently hosts her own show on WMCA radio in New York City.

United States:

Hank Rubin (California and the West Coast) contributes a monthly column answering wine questions for *Bon Appetit*. He is also a contributor to *Vintage* and *Food and Wine* magazines.

Richard Figiel (Eastern United States) is the editor of *Eastern Grape Growers and Winery News*.

We would also like to thank John Gottfried.